YUMAN AND YAQUI MUSIC

Da Capo Press Music Reprint Series

YUMAN AND YAQUI MUSIC

By Frances Densmore

DA CAPO PRESS · NEW YORK · 1972

Library of Congress Cataloging in Publication Data

Densmore, Frances, 1867-1957.
  Yuman and Yaqui music.

  (Da Capo Press music reprint series)
  Reprint of the 1932 ed.. which was issued as Bulletin
110 of Smithsonian Institution. Bureau of American
Ethnology.
    Bibliography: p.
    1. Indians of North America—Music. 2. Yuman
Indians. 3. Yaqui Indians. I. Title. II. Series:
U.S. Bureau of American Ethnology. Bulletin 110.
ML3557.D379   1972   784.7'51   72-1884
ISBN 0-306-70512-5

This Da Capo Press edition of *Yuman and Yaqui Music*
is an unabridged republication of the first edition
published in Washington, D.C., in 1932 as Bulletin
110 of the Bureau of American Ethnology, Smithsonian
Institution.

Published by Da Capo Press, Inc.
A Subsidiary of Plenum Publishing Corporation
227 West 17th Street, New York, New York 10011

YUMAN AND YAQUI MUSIC

SMITHSONIAN INSTITUTION
BUREAU OF AMERICAN ETHNOLOGY
BULLETIN 110

YUMAN AND YAQUI MUSIC

BY

FRANCES DENSMORE

UNITED STATES
GOVERNMENT PRINTING OFFICE
WASHINGTON : 1932

LETTER OF TRANSMITTAL

SMITHSONIAN INSTITUTION,
BUREAU OF AMERICAN ETHNOLOGY,
Washington, D. C., May 6, 1930.

SIR: I have the honor to transmit herewith a paper entitled "Yuman and Yaqui Music," by Miss Frances Densmore, and to recommend that it be published as a bulletin of the Bureau of American Ethnology.

Rspectfully,

M. W. STIRLING, *Chief.*

Dr. CHARLES G. ABBOT,
Secretary of the Smithsonian Institution.

FOREWORD

The songs of a group of tribes living along the Colorado River and in northwestern Mexico are here presented, the river culture affording an interesting contrast to the woodland, plain, high plateau, and desert cultures previously studied.[1] The Yuma and Mohave material was collected near Fort Yuma, Calif., the Cocopa material near Somerton in Arizona, a few miles from the Mexican border, and the study of the Yaqui music was made at Guadalupe village, near Phoenix, the entire research being made in 1922. A cremation was witnessed among the Yuma, and important dances were seen among the Cocopa and Yaqui.

The assistance of interpreters and prominent members of the Indian tribes is acknowledged with appreciation. The principal interpreter among the Yuma was Luke Homer, whose cooperation made possible the obtaining of old songs. During the work among the Cocopa it was necessary to employ two interpreters, Nelson Rainbow translating the Cocopa language into Yuma and Luke Homer translating Yuma into English. Katco'ra, a Yuma who spoke no English, assisted in the work by visiting the singers who lived at a considerable distance from Fort Yuma Agency, explaining the work to them, and bringing them to the writer. A similar service among the Cocopa was performed by Frank Tehanna, who also spoke no English. The Yaqui interpreter was Loretto Luna, a resident of Guadalupe village.

Four of the principal singers died before the publication of this material, and their bodies were cremated in the manner which they had described. The songs which they recorded for this work were undoubtedly sung on these occasions. These men were Charles Wilson, Joe Homer, and Peter Hammon (Yuma), and Clam (Cocopa).

---

[1] Chippewa Music, Bull. 45; Chippewa Music, II, Bull. 53; Teton Sioux Music, Bull. 61; Northern Ute Music, Bull. 75; Mandan and Hidatsa Music, Bull. 80; Papago Music, Bull. 90; Pawnee Music, Bull. 93; Menominee Music, Bull. 102, Bur. Amer. Ethn.; and Music of the Tule Indians of Panama, Smithsonian Misc. Colls., vol. 77, no. 11.

CONTENTS

ILLUSTRATIONS

LIST OF SONGS

1. ARRANGED IN ORDER OF SERIAL NUMBERS

2. ARRANGED IN ORDER OF CATALOGUE NUMBERS

2. Arranged in Order of Catalogue Numbers—Continued

2. Arranged in Order of Catalogue Numbers—Continued

Cata- logue No.	Title of song	Name of singer	Serial No.	Page
	Yuma Songs—Continued			
1237	Song concerning the quail_____	Katcora_____	98	168
1238	"I will make a flute"_____	Joe Homer_____	1	49
1239	"I have finished the flute"_____	_____do_____	2	50
1240	The Wonder-boy is born_____	_____do_____	3	51
1241	Game song (a)_____	Nelson Rainbow___	124	196
1242	Game song (b)_____	_____do_____	125	197
	Cocopa Songs			
1243	Opening song of the dance____ ._____	Numawàsoàt_____	99	170
1244	Song in the early evening (a)_____	_____do_____	100	171
1245	Song in the early evening (b)_____	_____do_____	101	172
1246	Song in the early evening (c)_____	_____do_____	102	173
1247	Song at about midnight (a)_____	_____do_____	103	174
1248	Song at about midnight (b)_____	_____do_____	104	175
1249	Song at about midnight (c)_____	_____do_____	105	176
1250	Song at about midnight (d)_____	_____do_____	106	177
1251	Song concerning the diver_____	_____do_____	107	178
1252	Song concerning the Pleiades_____	_____do_____	108	179
1253	Song in the early morning (b)_____	_____do_____	109	180
1254	Song in the early morning (c)_____	_____do_____	110	181
1255	Closing song of the dance_____	_____do_____	111	182
1256	The illness of the Superman_____	Clam_____	27	87
1257	The Superman sets an example_____	_____do_____	28	88
1258	The Superman grows weaker_____	_____do_____	29	89
1259	The Superman speaks_____	_____do_____	30	90
1260	The four corners of the earth_____	_____do_____	31	90
1261	The Superman dies_____	_____do_____	32	91
1262	Coyote comes to the cremation of the Superman.	_____do_____	33	92
1263	Coyote plans to seize the heart_____	_____do_____	34	93
1264	Buzzard tells the animals what to do_	_____do_____	35	94
1265	Coyote makes a request_____	_____do_____	36	95
1266	Coyote seizes the heart_____	_____do_____	37	96
1267	Coyote eats the heart_____	_____do_____	38	97
1268	Dancing song (a)_____	Mike Barley_____	115	187
1269	Dancing song (b)_____	_____do_____	116	188
1270	Dancing song (c)_____	_____do_____	117	190
1271	Dancing song (d)_____	_____do_____	118	191
1272	Dancing song (e)_____	_____do_____	119	192
	Yaqui Songs			
1273	Dancing song_____	Juan Ariwares____	83	156
1274	"The quail in the bush"_____	_____do_____	84	157
1275	"The little fly"_____	_____do_____	85	158
1276	Voices of the people _____	_____do_____	86	158
1277	"The deer are at play"_____	_____do_____	87	159

2. ARRANGED IN ORDER OF CATALOGUE NUMBERS--Continued

Cata-logue No.	Title of Song	Name of singer	Serial No.	Page
	YAQUI SONGS—Continued			
1278	"The deer and the flower"	Juan Ariwares	88	160
1279	"The summer rains"	-----do	89	161
1280	"The rising sun"	-----do	90	162
1281	"The bush is singing"	-----do	91	162
1282	The hunt (a)	-----do	92	163
1283	The hunt (b)	-----do	93	164
1284	The hunt (c)	-----do	94	164
1285	"The deer is dancing"	-----do	95	165
1286	Yaqui song	Jose Marie Umada	130	201
1287	Song of admiration	Anka Alvarez	129	200
	MOHAVE SONGS			
1288	Song of cremation legend	Billie Poor	39	99
1289	Bird dance song (a)	Leonard Cleveland	112	183
1290	Bird dance song (b)	-----do	113	184
1291	Bird dance song (c)	-----do	114	185
	MAYO SONG			
1292	Song of the deer dance	--Juan Ariwares	96	166

SPECIAL SIGNS USED IN TRANSCRIPTIONS OF SONGS

(· placed above a note shows that the tone was prolonged slightly beyond the indicated time.

·) placed above a note shows that the tone was given slightly less than the indicated time.

The letters A, B, C, and D are used to designate rhythmic periods consisting of several measures.

⌐‾‾‾‾‾¬ placed above a series of notes indicates that they constitute a rhythmic unit.

PHONETICS

Vowels have the continental sounds and consonants the common English sounds, except that—

ȧ is equivalent to English obscure *a*, as in the word *ability*.

c is a sound resembling English *sh*.

tc is a sound resembling English *ch*.

x is a sound resembling German *ch*.

ñ is a sound resembling English *ng* in the word *sing*.

NAMES OF SINGERS AND NUMBERS OF SONGS TRANSCRIBED

YUMA

Alfred Golding	26
Charles Wilson (Ampé'kwarau')[1]	24
Peter Hammon (Misȧhai'kwakiu)[2]	11
Mrs. Charles Wilson (Mavĕ', meaning snake)	7
Katco'ra	7
Joe Homer [3] (Jose Homer)	3
Nelson Rainbow	2

COCOPA

Numa'wȧsoȧ't	13
Clam [4] (Axlu'm)	12
Mike Barley (Api'lnoñne)	5

MOHAVE

Leonard Cleveland	3
Billie Poor	1

YAQUI

Juan Ariwares	13
Jose Marie Umada	1
Anka Alvarez	1

MAYO

Juan Ariwares	1
Total	130

[1] Died Sept. 10, 1929.   [2] Died Apr. 24, 1926.   [3] Died Dec. 22, 1929.   [4] Died in 1928.

CHARLES WILSON

YUMAN AND YAQUI MUSIC

By Frances Densmore

THE YUMAN TRIBES

The valley of the Colorado River was the early abode of a group of tribes known as the Yuman. The Colorado is one of the great watercourses of the country, and in a portion of its length it separates the States of Arizona and California. On either side are sandy stretches, high mesa rims, and barren mountains, beyond which lies an expanse of arid desert. The environment of the Yuman tribes shut them in and made them a unit, so that their civilization is distinct from that of the Pueblo or the Californian tribes. The gap between the southwesterners and the Yumans is profound as regards religion. There is no trace among the latter of kiva, altar, mask, offering, priest, initiation, fraternity, or color symbolism. These elements are replaced by the predominant factor of dreaming.[1]

The three Yuman tribes under present consideration are the Cocopa, Yuma, and Mohave. It is said that in 1604–05 the Cocopa lived 5 leagues above the mouth of the Colorado River, and that they extended into the mountains of Lower California. Thus they were confined almost exclusively to Mexican territory.[2] When the present work was in progress they were living in Sonora, Mexico, and southern Arizona, as well as in Lower California. North of the Cocopa are the Yuma, whose territory is the Colorado bottom land as far as the mouth of the Gila River. The juncture of these rivers is northeast of Yuma, Ariz. (pl. 2), and can be seen from that city. The illustration here presented was taken in 1900 by DeLancey Gill, from the site of the old territorial prison, located on the high promontory at the right of the bridge. (Pl. 3, a.) The ruins of the prison were standing in 1922. At this point the Colorado River divides Arizona and California. The Yuma live almost entirely on the west bank of the Colorado.

---

[1] Kroeber, A. L. Handbook of the Indians of California, Bull. 78, Bur. Amer. Ethn., p. 780.
[2] Handbook of American Indians, Bull. 30, Bur. Amer. Ethn., pt. 1, p. 319.

1

Above the Yuma, on the Colorado River, are the Mohave, their country being the valley which bears their name and is now in the three States of California, Nevada, and Arizona. The river civilization comes to a sudden stop with the Mohave, and above their country is the Eldorado Canyon, a bend of the river, and the vast gorge that culminates in the Grand Canyon. The Mohave are better known than the other Yuman tribes, and Kroeber states that "the most concentrated, energetic, and characteristic form of the river civilization of the past century or two has been that which it took among the Mohave."

In comparison with the Yuma they were "rather more venturesome and given to travel in far parts, and probably more active in their inward life, since their sacred places are known farther than Yuma influence penetrated." [3]

The Yuman Indians are "remarkable not only for their fine physical development, but living in settled villages with well-defined tribal lines, practicing a rude but effective agriculture, and well advanced in many primitive Indian arts. The usual Indian staples were raised except tobacco, these tribes preferring a wild tobacco of their region to the cultivated. None of the Colorado river tribes borrowed the art of irrigation from the Pueblo peoples; consequently their crops often suffered from drought. All of them depended more or less on the chase—the river tribes less, those of the interior more. Mezquite beans, piñon nuts, tornillas, and various seeds and roots were important articles of food. None of them were boatmen; in crossing rivers and transporting their goods they employed rude rafts, or balsas, made of bundles of reeds or twigs." [4]

According to Kroeber, "the Mohave . . . are distinctly yellowish in color, this color turning very dark brown by dirt and exposure to the sun.[5] This is in contrast to their eastern neighbors, the Papago, whose color is a reddish brown."

The town of Yuma, Ariz., is adjacent to the territory of the Yuma Indians. (Fig. 1.) It is on the eastern bank of the Colorado River and directly opposite, in California, is the high mesa on which Fort Yuma was formerly located. This is now the location of the United States Indian agency and school. (Pl. 3, a, b.) Looking west from the point of this mesa one sees the Colorado River and the flat land bordering it, dotted with the huts of the Indians; to the southwest are patches of scrubby trees, and at a considerable distance the cremation ground described in a subsequent chapter. Fort Yuma was established after the acquisition of California by the United

³ Kroeber, op. cit., p. 781.
⁴ Henshaw, H. W. Handbook of American Indians North of Mexico, Bull. 30, Bur. Amer. Ethn., pt. 2, p. 1011.
⁵ Kroeber, op. cit., p. 728.

States and the arrival of the overland tide of travel, but the Yuma offered no particular resistance to the white man. Their last military undertaking was an expedition against the Pima in 1858, which ended disastrously. The ancient enemy of all the Yuman tribes was the Maricopa, living along the Gila River.

The Yuma call themselves Kwichana, Kwichyana, or Kuchiana, the meaning of which is unknown to them. A Spanish designation

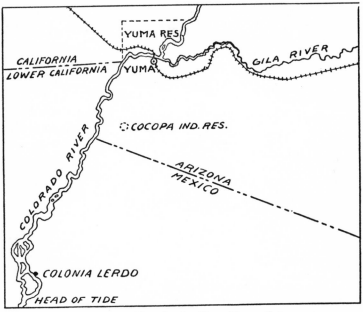

FIGURE 1.—Map showing Yuma Reservation

is Garroteros, clubbers, perhaps with reference to their mallet or pestle shaped war clubs. Father Kino wrote of the Yuma in 1690,[6] and the word "Yuma" appears first in his writings. The name is said to be derived from Yahmayo, meaning "son of the captain," which is seemingly the title of the son of the hereditary chief, contracted and applied to the tribe through misunderstanding by early Spanish missionaries.[7]

Father Kino and Father Garces encountered few difficulties among the Yuma, but two missions established later among the Yuma were destroyed in 1781, having been in existence only a year or two. The Spanish missionaries were massacred and the missions obliterated.

Early writers describe the Yuma as a fine people physically, and superior in this respect to most of their neighbors. They were brave and not averse to war, but generally stayed in their villages, where

---

[6] Doc. Hist. Mex., 4th s., vol. 1, p. 230.
[7] Bull. 30, Bur. Amer. Ethn., pt. 2, p. 1010.

they raised corn, beans, pumpkins, and melons by a crude form of agriculture. The population in 1853 was estimated at 3,000, and in 1929 there were 870 Indians under the school superintendency at Fort Yuma.

When visited by the writer in 1922, the Yuma were living in houses scattered over the reservation which had not been allotted in severalty. (Pl. 4, b.) Their dwellings in 1930 were still constructed chiefly of adobe and cottonwood poles, with thatched roofs. (Pl. 4, a.) A gathering of leading men of the tribe at an earlier date is shown in Plate 4, c. The land is the silt of the former river bed and occasionally has been overflowed.

The older men wear their hair long, often extending below the waist and matted in strands with bits of gum. (Pl. 5, a.) When desired, this is wound around the head like a turban. (Pl. 27, a.) Many of the younger men arrange their hair on top of the head in a high twist and cover it with a handkerchief. If they are traveling in a dust storm they tie a handkerchief across the lower part of the face to avoid breathing the dust. (Pl. 5, c.) Yuma women cut the hair slightly below the shoulders and wear it loose (pl. 5, b), cleaning it by means of wet clay placed on the hair at night and removed in the morning. (See p. 8.) The older men wear sandals in place of shoes, but carry them if the ground is muddy. Both men and women wear gay cotton mantels made by sewing together six or eight large red or blue handkerchiefs, all of the same pattern. This is shown in Plate 5, a, and in the portrait of Mrs. Wilson. (Pl. 31, b.) The foregoing applies to members of the tribe who have not fully adopted the white man's customs. On this, as on other reservations, there is a considerable number of young people attired in the manner of civilization and showing the results of education.

Two legends of the origin of the tribe were related. The oldest legend states that they came from a mountain farther up the Gila River, on the top of which is " a square place like a map," and the marks of little feet in the rock. All the tribes of Indians were sent from thence to various parts of the country, each being given what it would require in the place where it was to live.[8]

The Yuma were given the arrow weed with which to make their houses, and to use for many other purposes. They were given a place where they could fish and where there were many wild deer.

A legend said to be more recent in origin is that the Yuma traveled from a body of water and at every place they camped they made a fire. Traces of these fires can still be seen. It was said " the early Yuma were giants and the people have been gradually growing

---

[8] " The origin of mankind was attributed, as by all the Shoshoneans of southern California, to the north, whence a great divinity who still exists led the people to their present seats." (Kroeber, op. cit., p. 624.)

JUNCTURE OF COLORADO AND GILA RIVERS

a. BRIDGE ACROSS COLORADO RIVER AT YUMA

b. SITE OF FORT YUMA INDIAN SCHOOL

a. YUMA DWELLING, 1930

b. YUMA DWELLING, 1922

c. GATHERING OF LEADING MEN OF YUMA TRIBE

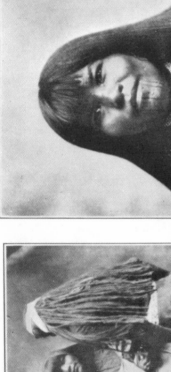

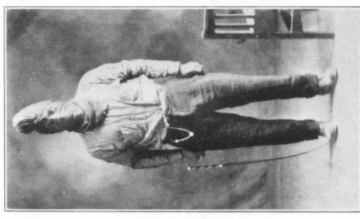

a. YUMA MAN AND WOMAN

b. YUMA WOMAN

c. YUMA MAN

smaller. They fought with giants, and there is a certain mountain
where they are said to have hung their enemies. On the face of
this mountain, at about evening, if one stands at a little distance
and looks at a certain angle it is possible to see picture writing and
at night one can hear low humming talk at that place."

The Yuma called the water "mother" and the sun "father," saying the sun called the earth up from below the water. They met and
kissed, and the sun drew back to the sky but the earth stayed where
it was. Mountains were left where the earth and sky drew apart.
They were the highest points of the submerged earth and remained,
becoming hard rock. Concerning this legend Kroeber says: "The
Shoshonean creation has been designated as a myth of emergence,
in the sense that mankind and all things in the world are born from
Mother Earth, with Sky or Night as father." This authority states
further that the Yuman tribes "add the fact that two brothers, the
creator and his death-instituting opponent, are born at the bottom of
the sea, and that the younger emerges blinded by the salt water. In
most Yuman accounts this concept of water origin is somewhat hesi-
tatingly blended with earth-sky parentage." [9]

The region near the site of Yuma is called Nĭ'mkwitiva'v, the
name said to have been given by a water animal called Bony-tail.
This mythical creature is said to still reside in the Colorado River
at a point where it flows between high cliffs and is now spanned by
an "ocean to ocean highway" bridge. (Pl. 3, a.) The current at
this point is very swift and the river deep, with many eddies. Bony-
tail stays there all the time and speaks for all fish. Thus when a
medicine man on his travels (in dreams) talks with Bony-tail, that
mythical creature becomes a human being and speaks for all the
living things in the water.

All the Yuman tribes cremate the dead and observe a strict taboo
concerning any mention of the dead after the Károk or memorial
ceremony (p. 76). An interesting example of this occurred during
the writer's work among the Cocopa. The building occupied as a
Government day school chanced to be vacant and was made available
for use, while at the same time a clerk from the Fort Yuma Agency
obtained certain data from the Indians. A goodly number were
gathered in the schoolroom, and routine questions were being read
in English by the agency clerk and interpreted to the assembled
Indians. Care had been taken in the form of these inquiries, but
inadvertently the interpreter mentioned the name of a dead man.
With one accord the Indians fled from the building. Mothers
wrapped their babies in shawls and fled, dragging small children by

⁹ Kroeber, A. L. Handbook of the Indians of California, Bull. 78, Bur. Amer. Ethn.,
pp. 788, 789.

the hand. The men hastened to the door as rapidly as possible. Looking from the window, we saw the bright shawls disappearing in all directions toward the Cocopa dwellings. Not understanding either the Yuma or Cocopa language, the writer was at a loss to explain this sudden change of mood on the part of the Indians, but the man who translated English into Yuma said (of the other interpreter), " He has done a terrible thing. He spoke the name of the dead. The Indians will not come back again to record any songs." The effort necessary to regain their confidence is apart from present consideration. The services of two interpreters were also required when the songs were recorded, one translating Cocopa into Yuma and the other translating Yuma into English.

The importance attached to dreams by the Yuman tribes has already been mentioned. Only one instance of a dream is contained in the present work, Wilson saying that in his treatment of the sick he used songs which his father had received in a dream (p. 101). Thus the Yuman tribes present a contrast to tribes previously studied in which many songs were received, actions prescribed, and a power said to be received in dreams by individuals. The dreaming of the Yuman tribes does not consist of visions in which spirits appear. The men, on the other hand, claim that they dreamed when unconscious infants and even prior to birth. " Singers sometimes say they first learned a song cycle in part and then dreamed the whole." [10] This is probably the meaning of a statement by Mike Barley, a Cocopa singer, that he " inherited these songs and could sing them without being taught." (See p. 186.)

The Mohave songs here presented were recorded by members of that tribe who live on the Yuma Reservation.

The Cocopa family group shown in Plate 6 is in the United States National Museum. This group was designed and installed by W. H. Holmes and the figures were modeled by U. S. J. Dunbar from photographs made in 1900 by DeLancy Gill. The label of this case, written by W. H. Holmes, contains a remarkably concise description of the tribe, stating that—

The Cocopa are limited agriculturists, raising corn on the flood plains of the Colorado River and securing much food from the grasses, mesquite, agave, screw bean, and cactus. They also fish in the Colorado River and the sinks formed by the overflows of the river and hunt rabbits and other small animals.

Their manufactures are the few articles required for their simple needs, such as water-cooling jars of porous pottery, cooking pots, etc., simple cord work. and weaving for nets and clothing, ornaments in shell, feathers, etc., for the head and neck.

---

[10] Kroeber, op. cit., p. 755.

Important household occupations are illustrated by the two women, one cleaning seeds with a basket and the other pounding grain in a wooden mortar. Water for drinking is cooled in a porous pottery jar set in the crotch of a tree where the air circulates freely, and the returning fisherman has his cup filled by the boy.

The pastimes of uncivilized peoples tend to some useful end, like the instruction of the boy in archery, which also furnishes amusement for the family. The sun shelter at the back serves also for the safe-keeping of the wicker storage basket, jars for seeds, digging sticks, and other implements of husbandry.

In the autumn of 1900 an extended exploratory trip for the Bureau of American Ethnology was led by Dr. W J McGee, then Ethnologist in Charge of the Bureau. Mr. DeLancey Gill accompanied the expedition as its photographer. This expedition was undertaken " for the purpose of completing researches relating to the aborigines of the Serian stock and at the same time carrying forward studies of neighboring tribes." [10a] Crossing the Gila River at Gila Bend, the party proceeded southward about 150 miles, passing the Ajo Mountains on their left, then traveled about 200 miles in a northwesterly direction to Colonia Lerdo, where they camped for a considerable time. (Fig. 1.) Many phases of Cocopa life observed and photographed in that vicinity have disappeared or been greatly modified since that time. (Pls. 6–18, a.) The arrow weed was so tall that it formed a jungle, through which Doctor McGee rode on horseback, following a narrow trail. (Pl. 7.) The men wore long hair, an old man of the tribe being shown in Plate 8, and a group of men with Doctor McGee appearing in Plate 9. The fourth man from the right is Frank Tehanna, mentioned in a subsequent paragraph.

Three types of dwellings were seen in 1900. The most primitive of these habitations was constructed chiefly of brush. (Pls. 10, 11.) Beside these dwellings may be seen storage bins for grain upon elevated platforms. A portion of the houses were made of earth and wattle, one dwelling being sealed because of the absence of its owner. A storage bin elevated only slightly above the ground is near this dwelling. (Pl. 12.) The larger dwellings were built of cottonwood poles, with roof of straw and clay, and an open shelter in front. (Pl. 13.) The largest house in the village was that of Chief Pablo Colorado, where a conference was held. (Pl. 14.)

Corn was cultivated in fields, harvested in a crude manner (pl. 15), and ground on a metate by the women (pl. 16). This constituted the principal article of food. The dead were cremated in their dwellings, together with all their personal belongings, the ground showing little trace of what had taken place. (Pl. 17.)

Frank Tehanna, a full-blood Cocopa, acted as guide for Doctor McGee's expedition and also assisted the writer in 1922. (Pl. 18, a, b.) He was about 30 years of age in 1900, and 6 feet 2½ inches

---

[10a] Twenty-second Ann. Rept. Bur. Amer. Ethn., pt. 1, pp. XI, XII.

in height. Mr. Gill designates him as " a trustworthy guide and a man of great physical strength." During the writer's study of Cocopa music he selected the singers and traveled many miles on horseback to explain the work to them and persuade them to record their songs. He returned, bringing the singer with him. (See p. 169.)

The writer's work was done in the Cocopa Day School, a neat building near an irrigation ditch. (Pl. 19, *a*, *b*.) The location is shown as " Cocopa Ind. Res." in Figure 1.

YUMAN CUSTOMS

Care of infants.—A " charm " for a baby consisted of a chain made from the four longest hairs in a horse's tail. This was hung around the child's neck and said to stop excessive drooling; it was also believed to cause the child to grow rapidly and be strong. A specimen of such a charm was obtained.

Education of children.—The Yuma began the instruction of their children before they were able to talk or understand what was said to them. The understanding of the child came gradually, and when it was 7 or 8 years old it had the teachings firmly in mind. These instructions were general in character, the expectation being that when the child was old enough he would use his own judgment in the application of the teachings to his manner of life.

Customs pertaining to food.—Rats were baked in hot ashes. Rabbits were sometimes skinned, cleaned, and stewed or roasted on hot coals. A refreshing drink used in summer was made as follows: A strip of bark about 12 inches wide was removed from a standing green willow tree. From this bark the inner layer was taken and a decoction made which was pink in color. It was sweetened and drunk either hot or cold.

Treatment of the sick.—Medicine men held a round white stone like a marble in their mouth when treating the sick. This was believed to bring success in their treatment.

There were household remedies in general use, but no magic was connected with them. For instance, the leaves of the greasewood were made into tea to break up a cold. The same decoction was used as a physic.

A remedy to prevent grayness and to keep the hair clean was made as follows: Mesquite gum and mistletoe were boiled and strained. To this liquid was added thick mud from the bottom of a certain lake. This was plastered on the hair at night and washed out in the morning. At about 10 o'clock one morning a Yuma woman was seen sitting in the sun washing this clay out of her hair.

Pictographs.—When a man reached a certain age he " put his mark on a rock for future generations." All the men in a family

GROUP OF COCOPA EXHIBITED IN THE UNITED STATES NATIONAL MUSEUM

TRAIL THROUGH JUNGLE OF ARROW WEED (1900)

OLD MAN OF COCOPA TRIBE (1900)

GROUP OF COCOPA WITH DR. W J MCGEE (1900)

COCOPA HABITATIONS CONSTRUCTED CHIEFLY OF BRUSH; ELEVATED STORAGE BINS FOR GRAIN (1900)

COCOPA HABITATIONS CONSTRUCTED CHIEFLY OF BRUSH; ELEVATED STORAGE BINS FOR GRAIN (1900)

COCOPA HOUSE OF EARTH AND WATTLE; STORAGE BIN SLIGHTLY ELEVATED ABOVE THE GROUND (1900)

COCOPA HOUSE OF COTTONWOOD POLES WITH ROOF OF STRAW AND CLAY (1900)

CONFERENCE AT HOUSE OF CHIEF PABLO COLORADO (1900)

COCOPA CORNFIELD AFTER HARVESTING (1900)

COCOPA WOMAN GRINDING CORN ON METATE (1900)

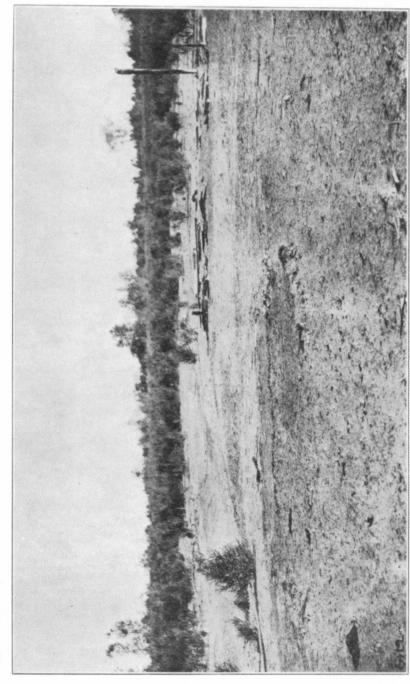

REMAINS OF COCOPA DWELLING AFTER CREMATION OF OWNER AND DESTRUCTION OF ALL HIS PERSONAL PROPERTY (1900)

b. FRANK TEHANNA. 1922

a. FRANK TEHANNA. 1900

a. IRRIGATION DITCH NEAR COCOPA DAY SCHOOL WHERE SONGS WERE RECORDED

b. STOCKADE FOR CATTLE AND SUN SHELTER NEAR COCOPA DAY SCHOOL

were said to have the same "animal mark." It was also said that a "kind of record" was kept on rocks, some of which remain near Laguna.

Hieroglyphics.—The Yuma formerly had a system of communication by means of drawings. For example, a certain sign was said to mean that an invitation to a certain sort of feast had been received and accepted. This consisted of parallel vertical lines, each crossed and recrossed by a curved line.

Paint.—For the decoration of pottery a paint was made of mesquite juice that hardens on the tree, mixed with mineral earth. In old times the Yumans daubed mineral paint on their clothing, resembling a dye in patterns and splotches. The young Cocopa women decorated their faces in elaborate designs. This custom was seen while the Cocopa songs were being recorded, the pattern on the face of one young girl being sketched. (Fig. 2.) The pattern on the cheeks was in blue, orange, and red; the pattern on the chin was entirely in red, and a butterfly was painted on the forehead. The decoration on the face was changed every day and sometimes during the day.

FIGURE 2.—Decorations painted on face of Cocopa girl

Tattoo.—When a girl is about 15 years of age she is tattooed with straight lines on her chin. (Pl. 5, *b*.) If thus tattooed she will "go straight to the spirit land when she dies," but without the tattoo "her spirit will wander around."

Courting customs.—The playing of the flute by young men is noted in the description of that instrument. Katcora said the girls used to play the jews-harp to attract the attention of the young men. One girl might play the jews-harp alone or two or three might play it together. He said, "If you are going along and hear this in some dark place you are bound to go there."

Preparation for marriage.—A girl was formerly taught household tasks when she was young, and it was required that she be proficient before she married. She must be able to prepare food, taking grain and grinding it on a stone. She then winnowed it in a basket, which must be held in a certain way so the chaff fell forward. Other tasks must be skillfully performed. The girls usually married when 16 or 17 years of age.

A young man must be a good farmer and have in storage a sufficient supply of watermelons, beans, pumpkins, and other vegetables to last almost a year.

At the present time parents occasionally "recommend" a young man, whom the girl afterwards marries. It was said the arrangement by the girl's parents is made only " for young girls who have not been out to dances." This indicates a general supervision by the parents, without any compulsion.

Old language.—The old songs of the Yuma Tribe are in an obsolete language, the words being repeated by rote. Mrs. Charles Wilson said that she remembered the numbers in this language, though she could not recall any words. The numbers counting up to 38 were phonographically recorded by this singer.

Dreams.—The Yuman belief in dreams differs materially from that of other tribes. (See p. 6.) Importance is attached to reticence on the subject, and it is said " if a man tells his dream it passes with the day," meaning that its power will depart. Joe Homer once had a dream in which he saw a mountain as white as snow, and at the top there was something circling and throwing out sparks. A voice commanded him to go to the top of the mountain. He went to the top of the mountain and came down and the voice said, " Well done." Homer told this dream to a medicine man, who said, " You have lost the power of your dream by telling it. Everyone knows it now. The power of that dream will never come back to you."

Hunting customs.—The Yuma sometimes held what was called a " burning hunt." They found a thick brush, burned it, and waited with bows and arrows to shoot whatever small animals ran from the fire. For this hunt they wore sandals with soles of heavy hide.

Belief concerning the dead.—It is said that four days after death the spirit takes a road toward the west until it comes to a place where its relatives who have previously died are waiting. They take it into a house and keep it four days. In that place it is early morning when the sun is setting here, and every day, early in the morning, the spirit is taken to a place where water is sprinkled on it, after which procedure it is bathed and incensed. The spirit is then free to go among its friends, who speak a different language, but live in about the same manner as people on the earth. (See Cremation and Károk.)

War customs.—The principal enemies of the Yuma were the Maricopa, who lived toward the north. They seem to have had no warfare with the Papago, their neighbors to the east. Their weapon was a very heavy club about 15 inches long, made of wood. (Pl. 20) The circumference of the head of the club was a little more than the grasp of a man's hand, and the thickness of the head was the width of a man's fingers. The stroke of the club was upward, directed toward the chin, and the weapon could be used with deadly effect, whether grasped by the handle, or, in closer conflict, held by the end.

The following information was given by Charles Wilson, who said that no songs were sung by a war party before its departure.

The warriors left the village quietly, all demonstration being reserved for their return. The medicine men who went with the warriors, however, had songs which they sang when treating the wounded. Many of the arrows were marked with messages. Such an arrow could be shot over the heads of the enemy and its message would summon help to a war party that was hard pressed. With the warriors were men who could " sing and bring on a sand storm." Such a song was preceded by a speech known only to the man making it and was immediately followed by the coming of the storm. These were " Lightning songs." (See p. 111.) When near the enemy the Yuma warriors disguised themselves by rolling in mud and then in sand. This caused their bodies to resemble the ground so closely that they could either work themselves forward without being seen or could lie motionless without attracting attention. It was said that on one occasion two scouts started from the vicinity of Yuma and went toward Ottman flat. One of them saw a cloud of dust anu knew that the Maricopa were approaching. He disguised himself and lay down next the brush beside the trail. The enemy passed without seeing him. Their leader was talking and the scout heard all he said. After the Maricopa had passed the scout carried the news back to his war party.

When an enemy had been killed it was the custom for four or five men to go with the medicine man who was to remove the scalp. This was a difficult task, as the skin of the entire head was removed. The informant said, "Anyone can see that if an ordinary person were to remove the skin it would not keep its shape." On reaching the body of the slain enemy the warriors circled around it and sang. Unfortunately all the songs of war were said to be lost, as it is many years since the Yuma went to war. The warriors stopped on the north side of the body, then on the west, south, and east sides, returning to the north side. The medicine man shook both legs of the corpse and rubbed them downward, then took the corpse by the legs and swung it around with the feet toward the north, west, south, and east. He dragged the body about a yard toward the east, stooped down, and put his face against that of the corpse as he sang certain songs. Then he began to " massage " the face of the corpse to loosen the skin. He dragged the body three times toward the east, thus making four stops, then he thrust his hand down into the ground, got some fine white sand and rubbed it on his face and hands, after which he seated himself beside the corpse and began his work. The first cut was from the inner corners of the eyes down to the chin, then around the neck. He removed the skin of the entire head with the ears attached. The warriors crowded around him as he swung the scalp to the height of his chest and dropped it on the ground, then he swung it a little higher and dropped it again. This was done four times, the medicine man finally lifting it as high as he could reach, while the crowd yelled at each elevation. The journey from the enemy's country usually required two days and a night. Some work on the scalp was done while the war party was returning and the work was continued after their return. Sand was rubbed on the inside of the hairy part of the scalp and the skin was treated like buckskin to soften it.

By the time they reached home the soft part of the ears had decayed and the medicine man "smashed" them in such a manner that they became dry; then he took a certain sort of willow bark and made a wrapping for the hair, leaving the rest of the head exposed. The warrior who killed the enemy put the scalp on the wall of his house and slept directly under it. In the course of two or three days the warrior found that the spirit of the slain enemy was going about, and he whispered to the spirit in the dark, telling him that the people around him were his friends and relatives, living close by, admiring him, and thinking of him every day and night. It was said this procedure usually "quieted down the spirit."

Preparations were then begun for "feasting the scalp" and for the victory dance. The warrior had a certain kind of pole made, about 4 feet high, for mounting the scalp. He took the scalp out during the night, washed it and combed the hair, and put "white chalk paint" on the face and hair, applying it with the palm of his hand. The manner of cutting the skin left an opening from the chin to the eyes, where the nose and mouth had been located. This slit was drawn together, the scalp was put on the pole, and the skin of the neck tied around the pole. In two or three days the warrior gathered all the people at his house and "feasted the scalp," or the "spirit of the enemy," and as long as the scalp was exposed to view the people came and feasted. The warrior repeated this every few days for a time. After this feasting was concluded the scalp was wrapped and again placed on the wall. Sometimes eagle feathers or other important feathers were placed with it. In the meantime the warriors who had killed enemies were subject to strict regulations. On the way home they were not allowed to touch their bodies with their hands but must use "scratch sticks" for that purpose. On arrival they must not go near their families for more than four days, though they might stay in the same house.[11] Every morning the warrior went early and jumped in the river; then he ate thin cornmeal gruel, vomited it, and drank water "to wash out his stomach." He ate nothing more during the day.

The victory dance was started by from one to three specially distinguished warriors who set the day for the dance, cleared a

---

[11] Cf. Papago Music, Bull. 90, Bur. Amer. Ethn., pp. 187–190.

space of ground, and made the arrangements. They "had a man there to sing songs in their honor," but it is said there is no one now living who knows these songs. The narrator (Charles Wilson) said he saw the dance and heard the songs when he was a young man.

The owner of the scalp took it to the place where the victory dance was in progress and stuck the pole in the ground. This was a signal that all the old men and women must join the dance, and at certain songs one of the dancers would take up the pole and carry it in the dance and return it to its place, after which another would do the same. Men, women, and young girls could carry the pole. The scalp was thus carried in the dance all night and the owner took it back to his home in the morning.

It was said to be a remarkable fact that no one could carry the scalp to or from the dance except the warrior to whom it belonged. It was said that frequently an "ordinary person" was sent to get a certain scalp and take it to a dance that was in progress. He tried to enter the house where the scalp was hung and if he succeeded in entering (which few were able to do) he wrapped the hair of the scalp tightly around his hand and started for the dance. But he had traveled only a short distance when he discovered that the scalp was no longer in his hand. He returned to find it, and to his surprise the scalp rose from the ground and stood upright, causing the man to scream with terror. While the scalp was in that position no one could touch it except the man to whom it belonged. The owner of the scalp could hold feasts for it whenever he desired, and take it to victory dances. When he died or was killed in war the scalp was "drowned" by throwing it into the river. If the warrior who took a scalp was killed before the party reached home the scalp he had taken was similarly "drowned."

Legends and song cycles.—The characteristic musical form among the Yuman tribes consists of cycles or series of songs which are interpolated in legends. (Cocopa, sayo', song; Yuma, scava'rr, song; scava'rrhuhai, singer.) Some of these legends can be related in about nine hours, while others are longer. The story is told in the common language of the present time and the songs, which are sung at intervals, are in the old language which is not understood by anyone, the words of the songs being learned with the melody and sung by rote. A general knowledge of their meaning is received by tradition. The words are said to embody a part of the narrative but they are not descriptive. The legend is usually concerning a journey and the songs appear to contain the choice bits and delightful little episodes, while the details of the journey are carried by the narrative. The songs appear to represent the poetry and the narrative the prose in a varied performance which gives great pleasure to these Indians.

It was said that a good story-teller would tell these stories whenever requested to do so. Thus at a gathering anyone might take up a collection, provide the basket and sticks, tobacco and some food, and get him to tell one of the stories. On such occasions the story-teller leads the singing and pounds on the basket, and those who know the songs " help him " by singing with him.

According to Kroeber, the journey described in these stories is almost invariably that of a single person or a pair of brothers, with or without a following. The journey is described as occupying two or three days, but is really a timeless life history of the hero or heroes, beginning with their coming into existence and ending with their transformation into an animal or landmark. The same authority states that " The plot is evidently a framework on which episodes . . . can be hung. We are thus face to face with a style of literature which is as frankly decorative as a patterned textile." " The same cycle is often sung quite differently by men not in any way connected with one another and the story appears to vary to an almost equal degree." The variance is said to consist in the selection of different minor incidents " with frequent recourses to remembrances of other singers and even diverse series." [12] For these reasons it was difficult, if not impossible, to secure an exact rendering of a cycle similar to the legends and their songs recorded among the Papago. It will be noted that the story of Pokohan is a combination of narratives by two men, and that the legend of the death of the Superman was recorded among both the Cocopa and the Mohave, the differences in the versions being noted. (See pp. 48–66, 85–100.)

The Yuma legends with songs enumerated to the writer were as follows:

1. Tcowi'ts (Bird) (songs 1–3).
2. Sakwa'tàxo'x (not recorded).
3. Ata'xmaili' (songs 4–14).
4. Hurau' (Lightning) (songs 44–56).
5. Akwa'k (Deer) (songs 57–82).
6. Hanyi' (Frog) (one song recorded but not transcribed).
7. Anya' (Sun) (not recorded).

Dancing took place only with the Deer songs.

The legends that were studied are described in connection with their songs. Joe Largo, who recorded a song of the Frog story (not transcribed), said it belonged to his father. In explanation he said, " The words represent the frog as starting on a journey toward the east and saying ' I will go east. I will get to Omi'kuda.' " No attempt was made to record all the songs of any cycle and the singer

---

[12] Kroeber, A. L. Handbook of the Indians of California, Bull. 78, Bur. Amer. Ethn., pp. 755, 756, 757.

was asked to choose a number from the portions sung at different parts of the night. It was the custom to divide the night into two parts (before and after midnight) and each half of the night had its songs. There was an order of the songs within these parts, certain songs being sung early in the evening, at about midnight, and " along toward morning."

In his description of Mohave customs, Kroeber states that " The Mohave have 20 narrative song cycles which they claim as their own, besides at least 10 more sung by doctors. Seven of the 20 are shared by one or more other tribes and are likely to be of foreign devising. The remainder, so far as known, are purely Mohave."

The number of songs in a Mohave cycle is indicated by his statement that " One narrator sang 33 groups of from one to five songs, 107 in all, in reference to the Nyohaive myth concerning war, which was sung without gourd rattle, the singer standing and leaning on his stick. Another series contains 169 songs in 83 groups." [13] Only one Mohave cycle received the attention of the present writer, this being outlined briefly in connection with song No. 39.

Dances.—The Yuman tribes appear to have few dances for pleasure. (Yuma, etcima'k, dance.) Dancing formed part of the Memorial ceremony and it was said that several dances were held before a cremation and a Memorial ceremony. The Deer dance and Corn dance were the only dances described in which the dancers encircled the musical instruments that accompanied the songs. In one dance the motion was in an elliptical path in front of the singers (p. 73) and in another (pp. 185, 186) the dancers and singers were in two parallel lines pushed backward and forward in the manner of the Ute bear dance described in Bulletin 75, page 57.

THE YAQUI TRIBE

A linguistic family other than Yuman is represented by the Yaqui and Mayo. These are the chief members of the Cahita, a group of tribes belonging to the Piman family and living chiefly in Sonora and Sinaloa, Mexico. It will be recalled that the Piman family has been represented in the present work by the Papago. (Bull. 90.) The name Yaqui is said to mean " chief river," referring to the Rio Yaqui.[14] Until recently the tribe lived along both banks of this river in Mexico. The first notice of the tribe is probably contained in the narrative of a Spanish expedition in 1531. The Yaqui defended themselves against attacks by the Spaniards during successive centuries. Perez de Ribas, a missionary among them

---

[13] Op. cit., pp. 761, 763, 785.

[14] The data concerning this tribe is condensed from the Handbook of American Indians, Bull. 30, Bur. Amer. Ethn., pt. 1, pp. 184, 185; pt. 2, pp. 991, 992.

between 1624 and 1644, says they were then agriculturists, cultivating not only maize but also cotton, which they made into cloth,
especially into the mantles worn in that region. They buried the
dead in graves. According to Dr. Aleš Hrdlička (Amer. Anthrop.,
VI, p. 8, 1904), "There is no organization among the Yaqui except in
that part of the tribe which lives practically free . . . neither do
they appear to have any secret societies." At the present time many
Yaqui live in southern Arizona and find employment on farms.

Numerous Mayo songs were offered for recording, but only one
is presented, No. 96. The word Mayo means "terminus," because
the Mayo River was the dividing line between this tribe and their
enemies. At an early time the Mayo occupied 10 towns and were
the most populous of all the tribes of Sinaloa. They cultivated the
soil, raised sheep and domestic birds, and made woolen shawls. The
Mayo were peaceable people, in contrast to the warlike Yaqui, and
their language differs only in dialect from the language of the
Yaqui.

YUMAN AND YAQUI SONGS

The material under consideration comprises the following groups:
Yuma, 80 songs; Cocopa, 30 songs; Mohave, 4 songs; Yaqui, 15
songs; Mayo, 1 song.

The Yuman tribes are represented by a variety of songs, while
the Yaqui and Mayo are represented only by songs of the Deer
dance cycle and a few modern songs which show a Mexican influence.

The musical customs of these tribes are peculiar, and for that
reason an observation of the singing at gatherings of Indians was of
unusual importance. Many Yuma songs, not recorded, were heard
during the cremation ceremony, the Cocopa songs were heard during
a gathering of the tribe near the Mexican border, and the Yaqui
songs during a celebration of Good Friday, near Tucson, Ariz., in
1920, and during the celebration of Thursday, Friday, and Saturday of holy week at Guadalupe Village, near Phoenix, in 1922. On
each visit to the Yaqui villages the writer remained for several
hours beside the singers. More than 160 Yuman and Yaqui songs
were recorded, but the number presented is 130. The remainder
were studied and found to contain the same peculiarities.

YUMAN SONGS [15]

The principal Yuman songs are in cycles. There is dancing in a
few but not all of these cycles, which require an entire night for performance, each part of the night, as already stated, having its proper

---

[15] This subject is considered in a different manner by George Herzog in The Yuman
Musical Style, Jour. Amer. Folk-Lore, vol. 41, No. 160, pp. 183-231, April–June, 1928.

songs. In the Corn dance, Memorial ceremony (Károk), and probably in other classes of songs, the songs are in pairs, the second having
no words. In a majority of the recorded songs the words are in an
obsolete language, which occurs only in the songs, and the meaning
of which is known only to the singers. The meaning of the Károk
songs is lost entirely. The only way for a man to learn the old songs
is to be a " helper " when an old man who knows the songs is singing
them. As the singing usually continues all night for several consecutive nights it is possible for the " helpers " to learn the songs in this
manner. It is said that no songs are being composed or received in
dreams at the present time.

The Yuma announced the subject of a song after it had been sung.
The Sioux announced the subject before singing the song. The
Chippewa made no announcement.

Unusual difficulties surround the transcription and analysis of
Yuman songs. The form of a melody is determined to some extent
by the words of the song, and the present material contains many
songs connected with legends and embodying part of the narrative.
The words of these songs, as already stated, are in a language which
is obsolete, the singer repeating the words by rote. The integrity of
these words was proven by the rendition of No. 109 by a Cocopa and
a Yuma, the words as well as the melody being the same on the two
phonograph cylinders. It is not practical to undertake the placing
of such words or syllables beneath the notes of a transcription.

These melodies, although connected with narratives, differ from the
legend songs of the northern Ute which are classified as " rudimen-
tary." (Cf. Bull. 75, Bur. Amer. Ethn., pp. 200–204.) The Ute Indians stated that these songs were improvised, yet certain songs contain a characteristic of the animal mentioned in the story; for example, the slowness of the bear and the agility of the prairie dogs.
An interesting and somewhat different sort of narrative song was
recorded by the Tule Indians of Panama. (Cf. Music of the Tule
Indians of Panama, p. 3.) The Tule songs were improvised, like the
Ute songs, but each had a distinctive rhythmic phrase repeated often
and reflecting the character of the song.

The Yuman songs appear to be in a form that is intermediate between the Ute of northern Utah and the Tule Indians of Panama.
Many of these songs consist of several divisions designated as "rhythmic periods " (see table 17, p. 209), and there are rules for the repetition of these periods. On studying the phonographic records we
find, however, that the opening phrases often were sung a larger number of times than prescribed by rule. Eleven repetitions of the opening phrases were counted in some songs, but the transcription contains only the usual mark for repeat. Furthermore, a cylinder often

contains a seemingly impromptu repetition of short phrases in irregular order, after the rendition shown in the transcription. The "rules" for the form of these songs are interesting, but apparently were not considered binding upon good singers. A study of variations from the rules was not undertaken, the present work being concerned with the more constant phases of the music.

In many instances a long duration of singing was transcribed in addition to the material presented, and no orderly sequence of phrases could be discovered. This portion of the cylinder appears to contain an impromptu use of the previous thematic material and is noted in the descriptive analyses. It is said that the Károk songs, after being sung four times, could be ended at any point in the melody, and in those songs the ending of the transcription is at a measure satisfactory to the ear. This is believed to be the end of the song. An arbitrary ending occurs also in the transcriptions of certain Yuma songs recorded by Wilson, and in one Mohave song. Four of these are Wilson's personal songs for the treatment of the sick, and the Mohave song was used for the same purpose. In this connection we recall that in other tribes it is a frequent custom for doctors to disguise their songs as well as their remedies, making it difficult, if not impossible, for others to learn them. The medicine songs of Wilson bear a peculiar resemblance to the Tule songs already cited. In one of these songs (No. 42) the entire cylinder was transcribed. Wilson was singing when the end of the cylinder was reached, with no evidence of being near the end of his performance. The other songs with this designation are legend songs recorded by Wilson. The singers realized that it was impossible to record a complete performance of each song, so they endeavored to condense the performance into the space of a phonograph cylinder.

The characteristic form of Yuman songs, as indicated, is a "period formation" with one, two, or occasionally three long periods and a short period containing the more pleasing part of the melody. This peculiar form was first noted in the songs of the Tule Indians of Panama. It occurred with frequency in 130 Acoma, Isleta, and Cochiti songs studied by the writer, and was also found in the songs of the Big Cypress Swamp Seminole in southern Florida. In each tribe the songs having this form were said to be very old. In describing the form of Yuman songs the interpreter said, "There is always a chorus near the end of a song that goes up higher." He said it is the custom that "the song shall be sung four times and the chorus twice," also that "if the chorus is sung a third time the ending is on a high note." The term "chorus" is derived from a knowledge of the white man's songs and indicates a pleasing part of the song but not a change in the number of singers. It usually contains about

eight measures and is not repeated. The other portions of the song
are sung from 2 or 3 to 11 times and are accurately repeated. Emphasis should be placed upon the fact that if a phrase in the transcription is repeated it is given with exactness, showing it is clear in
the mind of the singer, though other phrases in the song may bear a
close resemblance to it. The part of the melody designated as the
" chorus " will be recognized in many transcriptions. It is the second
or third period and is higher in pitch and more pleasing in melody
than the preceding portion. In some instances the return to the
earlier portions of the song is indicated as a " repeat."

The melodic form of these songs is in sections or periods which
are designated by the letters A, B, C, and D. Rhythmic units occur
in many songs and are designated by brackets above the notes, as in
the songs previously transcribed.

A peculiarity found in the songs of Yuman cycles and also in the
Yaqui cycle of the Deer dance is a pause of indefinite length, designated as " pause ad lib." The duration of this pause did not conform to the metric unit of the song but was usually about a measure
and a half or two measures. This pause occurs about halfway
through the transcription, but is nearer the end of the performance,
as the repeated portion in the first part was sung at least four times.

A further peculiarity of these songs lies in the frequent occurrence
of rests, the tone before a rest being ended in a definite manner.
The Indian tribes under observation differ in the use of a rest in
their songs, many singers being able to take breath in a manner
which is imperceptible to a listener. A rest occurred in 13 per
cent of 340 Chippewa songs, in less than one-half of 1 per cent
of 240 Sioux songs, in more than 11 per cent of 110 Ute songs, and
in 19 per cent of 110 Mandan and Hidatsa songs. (Cf. Bull. 80,
p. 4.) When rests occur in Indian songs they frequently are in the
middle of a phrase, not at the end of a phrase or a word, for the
purpose of taking breath.[16] Songs recorded by younger Indians
occasionally contain short rests which can be identified as pauses
for breath, partly because the location of the rest differs slightly
in the several repetitions and also because the tone preceding the rest
is not ended with crispness. A rest in the old Indian song occurs
uniformly in all renditions and is given with careful clearness.

No songs are being composed by the Cocopa at the present time.
Probably this is also true of the Yuma. Mention has been made
of a resemblance between Yuman and Pueblo songs. A further
resemblance consists in the gradual changing of the pitch during

---

[16] The same peculiarity has been noted in the music of India. " Rests are seldom
written . . . in any of their songs, at any rate not, as we should, on account of the
words. . . . They appear to take breath when they want to take it, not at the end of
words." (Fox Strangways, Music of Hindostan, pp. 192–193.)

the singing of a song. This has occasionally been noted in other tribes but regarded as incidental, or a personal idiosyncrasy, since an overwhelming majority of the phonograph records show a maintenance of pitch on the principal melody tones which would be creditable to a singer of our own race. One singer of the Yuma Tribe (Charles Wilson) gradually lowered the pitch during the renditions of some of his songs. This lowering of the pitch can not be shown graphically unless a pitch indication is placed before practically every note. In the belief that such signs would add to the difficulty of observing more important characteristics this peculiarity is mentioned in the descriptive analysis. The former custom of keeping the transcription as simple as possible is continued in the present work.

A peculiarity of Chippewa music was the difference in tempo of voice and drum, a comparative table showing that the tempo of voice and drum was the same in only 36 per cent of 214 songs recorded with accompaniment. (See Bull. 53, Table 22, p. 33.) As an interesting contrast we note that the tempo of voice and drum was the same in 89 per cent of 65 Ute songs recorded with accompaniment. (See Bull. 75, Table 22, p. 51.) In Yuman songs the tempo of voice and drum or rattle is always uniform and the two are synchronous, but the rhythm of the accompanying instrument is not always the same during the entire song. In a majority of instances the rattle was shaken rapidly before the song was begun and during its opening measures. The change to a rhythmic shaking of rattle was not so abrupt as in the Pawnee songs (see Bull. 93, p. 29), but the rhythm in many songs was not clearly defined until measures 6 and 10. Several examples of interrupted rhythms in drum or rattle are transcribed. The accompanying instrument was discernible throughout the entire performance.

An important peculiarity of Yuman songs is the variety in the rhythm of the accompaniment. The songs previously recorded have been accompanied by drum or rattle in a few simple rhythms or in strokes of equal force without rhythm. Thus 38 per cent of 475 songs of various tribes were accompanied by rattle or drum in unaccented quarter or half notes, the beat of the drum corresponding to these note values in the melody. (Bull. 80, Table 18, pp. 25–26.)

The Yuman songs show a remarkable variety in the form as well as the rhythm of their accompaniment, the songs being accompanied by percussion, by rattles, by a nasal grunting, and by pounding of the feet, each form of accompaniment being used with a certain sort of song, or with a certain cycle. The basket drum (see p. 24) may be beaten with the palm of the hand, with one or more willow sticks, or with one or two bundles of dry arrowweed. The rattles comprise a small gourd rattle, a large gourd rattle, a dew-claw rattle, and a rattle made from a spice box. The nasal grunting is used with game songs. In this peculiar accompaniment the breath is forced into the nose by a spasmodic contraction of the chest, producing a sound resembling " huh, huh," in exact time to the music. Songs connected with the cremation or the Károk are accented by stamping first one foot and then the other on the ground. What may be termed a " foot accompaniment" is used also in the " Human being dance."

In the following list it will be seen that the basket is struck with the palm of the hand in only two song cycles. The singer of the frog songs held a willow stick in his right hand and struck the basket simultaneously with the stick and with the palm of his left hand. The accompaniment of the Deer dance songs is described on p. 131. Songs of all these cycles were recorded.

Legend	Accompaniment
Concerning a bird	Basket struck by bundle of arrowweeds.
Concerning a coyote	Basket struck by bundle of arrowweeds.
Concerning a deer	Basket struck by palm of hand and willow sticks.
Concerning the lightning	Basket struck by willow sticks.
Concerning the frog	Basket struck by palm of hand and willow sticks.
Corn dance	Large rattle.
A social dance	Large rattle.

The large gourd rattle was used for all social dances and for the songs called " Bird songs," which formed a class by themselves. It was said that the last man who knew all these songs died a few years ago. The singing and dancing lasted all night, and it was said there were usually five or six divorces after this dance. " Bird songs " were sung also by the Cocopa and the Mohave. A small gourd rattle was used by a medicine man in his personal songs.

The " spice-box rattle " was used in the Károk and Human Being dance, and the dewclaw rattle was used only in the cremation ceremony.

In tribes studied prior to the Papago there did not appear to be a prescribed degree of loudness for the singing of certain songs. In a dance of the Cocopa there was a special mannerism for the songs that were sung in the early evening (Nos. 100, 101, 102). These songs were always begun softly and then increased in volume. The songs of the Pokohan legend were always sung very softly.

Other peculiarities of Yuman songs are discussed in connection with the comparative tables of analysis on pages 37–40.

YAQUI SONGS

The Yaqui songs herewith presented were recorded in Guadalupe village, near Tempe, Ariz. The Yaqui came from Mexico and took up their abode at this place many years ago, but are not under the Government of the United States. They are governed by a chief who has several captains under him and a policeman who appears very efficient. The village is set in the midst of the desert and is a compact little settlement, the houses being set in rows, along two extremely wide streets. (Pl. 21, a, b.) The Yaqui interpreter, Loretto Luna, and his child are shown in front of his house. (Pl. 21, c.) The village well, operated by a windmill, is in the middle of one of these streets. There are fences in front of most of the houses and narrow alleys in the rear. The fences are made of the ribs of the saguaro cactus, set upright and fastened together, usually bound with wire. In some instances the fences are about 4 feet high with a gate and the cactus stalks are placed so close together that they form a stout paling. The streets and yards are of hard bare ground and reasonably clean. No attempt at cultivating the ground was observed. The houses were varied in structure and usually consisted of two or more inclosed rooms and an "outdoor room" with roof but with the sides only partly inclosed, leaving one side or parts of two sides open. The better class of houses were of adobe with roofs of earth resting on cactus ribs; others were of cactus ribs calked with adobe and others had sides formed of overlapping pieces of tin or wood, these pieces having the appearance of having been gathered from rubbish heaps.

The population of the village may be estimated at about 150. The men earn a scanty living by hauling wood or working for farmers in the vicinity. They are evidently very poor, but the atmosphere of the village is that of content and good order. Father Lucius, a Franciscan missionary monk, has built an adobe church in the village and established a day school. Near the church is a chapel, in front of which the Deer dance was given in 1922. (Pl. 21, d.) The school teacher is a woman who does not live in the village nor go among the houses to form the acquaintance of the people. She is, however, successful in maintaining the work among the children, as is shown by the enrollment of more than 50 pupils. Thus the thought of the future members of the tribe is being formed along proper lines, but the customs of the older people are not under surveillance.

The songs were recorded in a bakehouse adjoining the house of the policeman. (Pl. 21, a.) A corner of the bakehouse is seen in the illustration which shows the house and one of the sides of the "outdoor room." The bakehouse had one small window and an opening into a huge adobe oven resembling a kiln, in which the bread was baked. The dome of the oven can be seen at the right. The room was furnished only with a long table on which the bread was mixed. The phonograph was placed near the door, and about 30 Indians gathered outside to watch the process of recording and listen to the results. This made it impossible to make an intensive study of the Deer dance and its history, but the condition was unavoidable. The three singers who made the records represented the two sorts of Yaqui music, and the interpreter was Loretto Luna, an intelligent Yaqui who spoke excellent English.

Yaqui music is of two sorts, one of which appears to be native and the other influenced by Mexican or Spanish. The former is accompanied by native instruments and the latter accompanied by the guitar, violin, harp, or other stringed instruments. The people insist that the latter sort of music is also Yaqui and that "Mexican songs are different." The pleasure of the young men in their musical performances was shown by the following incident: The writer, on going to the village one morning, heard concerted music in one of the houses. In reply to an inquiry a Yaqui said, "The young men are playing. They often play like that all day." The house was of adobe with two rooms and the musical performance was in the second room with the door closed. The young men consented to open the door, revealing a room that was lighted only by a very small window. In the semidarkness several young men were playing the violin, one double bass adding to the effect. They were playing one tune after another without printed notes and apparently improvising part of the time. The music was pleasing in style, somewhat plaintive, and resembled that heard at the "Mexican dances" in other parts of southern Arizona. The musical instruments used at the Good Friday celebration at Tucson are mentioned on page 27.

As already stated, two distinct types of songs are now used by the Yaqui, the old songs which are said to be strictly native and the modern songs which show a Mexican influence. The Deer dance songs (Nos. 83 to 95) are examples of the old songs and were accompanied by a gourd rattle. A Mayo song of the same dance is presented (No. 96). Two examples of the modern songs (Nos. 129, 130) were accompanied by the guitar. Other modern songs were recorded, but the resemblance between them was so marked that the songs here presented were considered sufficient.

Several Yaqui Deer dance songs contain the long pause which characterizes the Yuman song cycles, but they do not have the same period formation. The Mayo song was recorded by a Yaqui and contains no striking peculiarities. Other Mayo songs were offered but not recorded.

In the modern Yaqui songs we note a fluent melody and a glissando in both ascending and descending progression.

The transcription of Yuman and Yaqui songs is on the pitch of the phonograph record except that songs having F sharp as their keynote are transcribed in the key of F in order to simplify the notation.

A limited number of songs are classified as irregular in tonality as they appear to be pure melody, without an apparent keynote.

YUMAN MUSICAL INSTRUMENTS AND THEIR USE

The only drum used by the Yuman tribes is a basket (kwĕnxo'), struck with implements or with the palm of the hand. As among the Papago, the sound of this accompaniment was not sharp enough for phonograph recording, so a pasteboard box was substituted and beaten with a small stick during the recording of the songs. The basket is usually obtained from the Papago, as the Yuma are makers of pottery rather than of baskets. As stated in Papago Music (Bull. 90, p. 3), this is an ordinary household basket, overturned on the ground when in use as a drum. Such a basket obtained among the Papago was 16½ inches in diameter and 5½ inches in depth. The basket used in recording Yuma songs was 13 inches in diameter and 4 inches in depth. The Papago struck the basket with the palms of the hands or stroked it with a short, flat stick. The Yuma beat upon the basket with the palm of the hand and also with willow sticks and bundles of arrowweed. (Pl. 22.)

The willow sticks (nyima' lwakwĭt plu.) used with the basket were said to be two "spreads" from the thumb to the end of the second finger in length and about an inch in diameter, and a singer held a pair of the sticks in his right hand. The sticks were found to be 15 inches long.

The bundles of arrow weed (i'sav, arrow weed; isa'vaota'p, bundles of arrow weed) were 25¼ inches in length, tied near the butt end where the bundle was 1½ inches in diameter. The bundles used by Golding were examined and found to contain 10 rods or stems of the weed in one bundle and 12 in the other. A singer who uses these arrow weeds a great deal has a pair of bundles which he carries with him wrapped in a cloth when he expects to sing. Golding followed this custom when coming to record his songs. At present the principal singer and his assistant each have one of these bundles. In former times the principal singer had two assistants.

The number of baskets depended upon the number of dancers. If the circle were small and only one basket were in use, two, three, or four men might beat upon the basket with willow sticks, but only two could beat it with bundles of arrow weed, as they were so much larger. Three baskets were formerly used in the Deer dance (see

YUMA WAR CLUB

a. HOUSE WHERE SONGS WERE RECORDED

b. HOUSE IN YAQUI VILLAGE

c. LORETTO LUNA AND CHILD IN FRONT OF HIS HOUSE

d. CHAPEL IN FRONT OF WHICH DEER DANCE WAS GIVEN

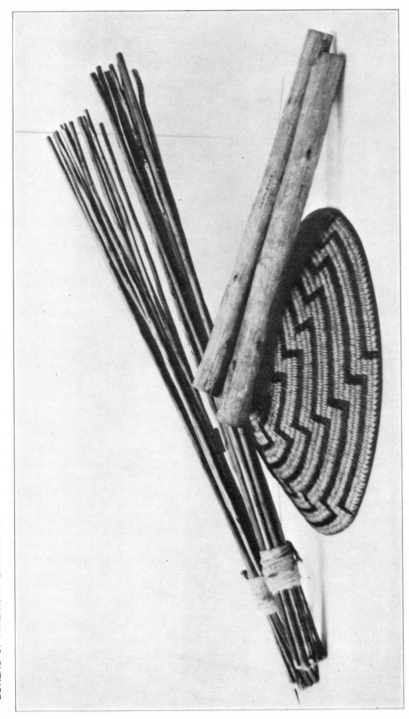

BASKET USED AS DRUM, WITH COTTONWOOD DRUMSTICKS AND BUNDLES OF ARROW WEED USED AS DRUMSTICKS

COCOPA GOURD RATTLE

MOHAVE GOURD RATTLE

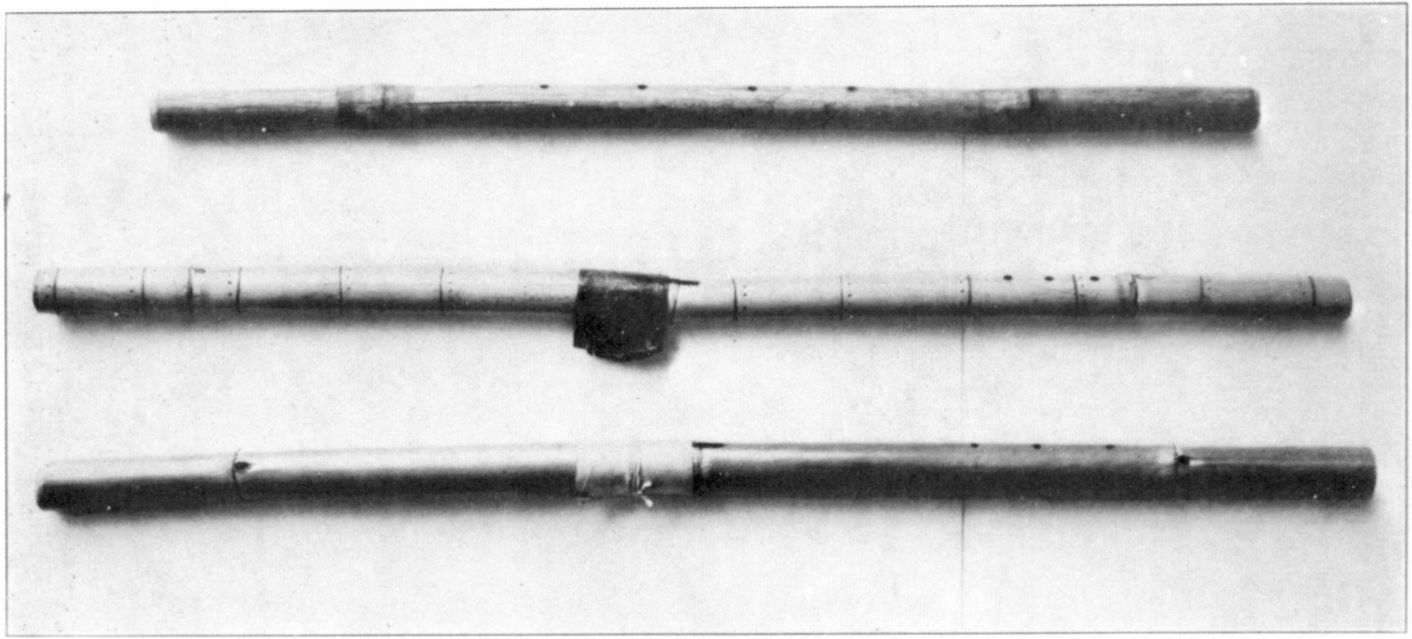

Yuma Transverse and Vertical Flutes

p. 155), and four singers were seated at each basket, one of them being the leader and using the bundles of arrow weed.

The Yuma, Cocopa, and Mohave used a gourd rattle (Yuma, axma'l; Cocopa, hulima'). The Cocopa songs were recorded with a large gourd rattle painted red. (Pl. 23.) A smaller gourd rattle was used by the Mohave when singing the Bird songs. (Pl. 24.) The Mohave rattle was decorated with a pattern of diagonal lines which was said to have no meaning. Inside this rattle were about thirty tiny balls of pottery made especially for this purpose and baked in the fire. The handle was of ironwood, fastened in place with gum made by mashing and cooking arrow weed stalks and adding red paint. This rattle was also used with the Támànt songs.

The "spice-box rattle" was made of a small tin box pierced by a stick which formed the handle. In the box were BB shot. These rattles were used in the Human Being dance and were shaken by 8 or 10 men who sat in a row on a bench. The leading singer sat in the middle and used a rattle with more shot in it, giving it a louder tone. This is similar to the rattles made of thin wood or birchbark and used by the Chippewa in the Midewiwin, or Grand Medicine Lodge.

The dewclaw rattle used at cremations is described in connection with that ceremony (p. 42).

A rattle consisting of a string of cocoons containing small pebbles was wrapped around the knee of the leading Deer dancer. (See pp. 155, 156.)

FLUTES AND THEIR MUSIC

The legendary origin of the flute among the Yuma is described in the chapter concerning the origin of the cremation (pp. 48–66).

The Yuma have two sorts of flute made of cane, commonly called bamboo. (Pl. 25.) These are the transverse (wǐlwǐl'axtü') and the vertical or end-blown flute (wǐlwǐl'tělhuku'p). In making the former flute the natural divisions of the cane are removed in the entire length of the tube and the " mouthpiece " is formed by the player's lips, the instrument being held horizontally toward the right, and the sound directed across the edge of the tube. Such a flute was played for the writer. The performance was not recorded phonographically, but the tones were those of a major third with its intermediate tone. The phrases appeared to be repeated in irregular order as in the usual playing on primitive flutes, and the rhythm was that of double time. It was said that additional tones could be played on other flutes of the same sort. The native names of both flutes are based upon " wilwil," which is the name of a small bird. It was possible to obtain the instrument, which is about 27¼ inches long and has four finger holes, placed slightly nearer one end than the other. These are respectively 11, 12⅝, 14⅛, and 15 inches from the end to which they are nearest, and the holes are slightly smaller than in the vertical flute. It was said this flute could be blown at either end. The player, George Escalanti, stopped the holes with the first and second fingers of each hand.

In making a vertical or end-blown flute the natural divisions of the cane are not all removed. One of these is left midway the length of the cane for use in making a " whistle head." Two specimens of this flute were obtained and the music of one was phonographically recorded. George Escalanti (pl. 26, *a*), who made these flutes, is commonly known as Captain George and is a man of high character, respected by both Indians and white people. His title is derived from long service as captain of Indian police on the

Yuma Reservation. The flute on which he played was without decoration. The two which he made for the writer were decorated with small brown dots. He said that the length of the end-blown flute was " three spreads of the hand from the thumb to the tip of the second finger and about two-thirds more." The length of the specimen is 28 inches. The sound hole is cut above the " partition " inside the cane, midway its length. It is about 1¼ inches long and three-sixteenths of an inch wide, and across the upper end is wrapped a piece of brown paper secured by a string. This covers about one-fourth of an inch of the opening. The tone may also be controlled by the player's finger, partially covering the hole. Captain George said that after cutting the sound hole he drew a line from the sound hole to one end of the cane, placed the other end in his mouth as if to blow it, and marked places for three finger holes where his fingers rested most conveniently. These finger holes are 4¾, 5⅞, and 7 inches, respectively, from the " speaking end " of the flute.

In old times the Yuma had no love songs, but two or three young men played these flutes in unison to attract the attention of the

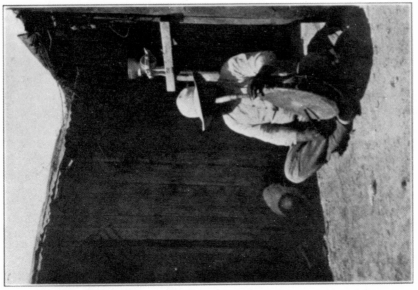

b. YAQUI PLAYING FLUTE AND DRUM AT THE SAME TIME

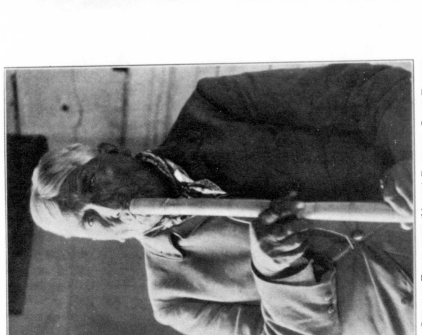

a. GEORGE ESCALANTI (YUMA) PLAYING CANE FLUTE

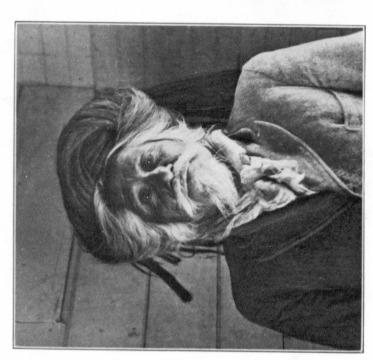

b. CLAM (COCOPA)

a. KATCORA (YUMA)

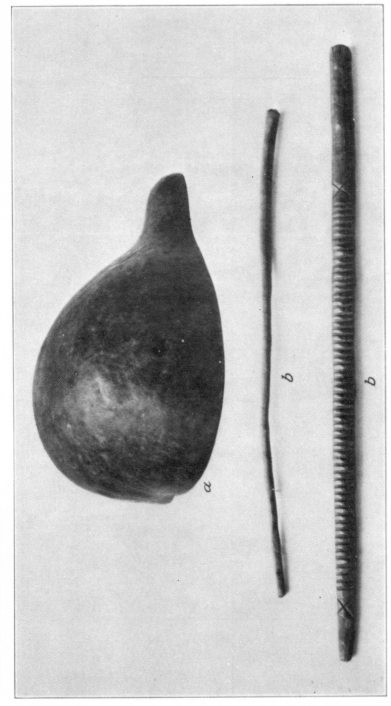

YAQUI RASPING STICKS AND HALF GOURD USED AS RESONATOR

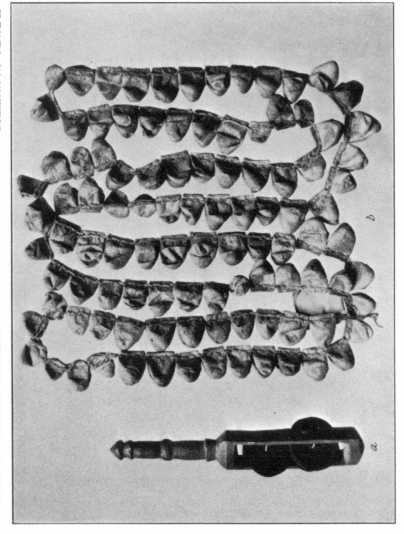

YAQUI RATTLES

a, Used in Deer dance; *b*, worn in Deer dance.

young girls. It was said "the girls sat and listened, and marriages had been known to result."

Two consecutive records were made by George Escalanti, playing the vertical flute. (Pl. 26, a.) In both instances the intonation was generally what would be called "good" if produced by a manufactured instrument. It is difficult to play a cane flute, and the phrases were at times disconnected but the tones were the same in all. The first record shows a tone with the major second and major third above it, played in various sequences; the second shows the same tone with the minor second and minor third below it, played in various orders. The records closely resemble those of the Papago flute (Bull. 90, pl. 1, pp. 212, 218). Similar instruments are used by the Kamia.[16a]

YAQUI MUSICAL INSTRUMENTS AND THEIR USE

Two types of musical instruments were heard in the Yaqui village of Guadalupe, corresponding to the old and modern types of music. The Deer dance was accompanied by instruments of both classes. On the right side of the line of dancers were several violins, while on the left were the old, native instruments consisting of half-gourds placed on the surface of a pan of water and struck with a stick, also placed on the ground and struck with a stick, and used as a resonator for rasping sticks. (Pl. 28.) The leading dancers carried rattles made of flat pieces of wood between which circular disks were set in such a manner that they jingled. (Pl. 29, a.)

In a Yaqui house the writer saw a small harp of native manufacture and heard it played. The instrument was said to be about 25 years old. It was 3 feet high, had about 30 strings, and was held in a horizontal position when played, the lower end resting on a brace which formed part of the instrument. The player was seated and held the instrument between his knees, the position making the strings almost horizontal. The instrument was well tuned and the music resembled that of the "Mexican dances." These small harps were said to be a characteristic instrument of the Yaqui.

Small drums and short reed instruments like "shepherds' pipes" were used in the celebration of Good Friday at Tucson, Ariz., in 1920.

In the yard of a Yaqui house a man named Manuel Ayala was seen playing a flute and drum at the same time. (Pl. 26, b.) The flute consisted of two separable sections and was 14 inches long. It had only two sound holes and the distance from the second (lower) sound hole to the end of the flute was about 7 inches.

[16a] Gifford, E. W. The Kamia of Imperial Valley, Bull. 97, Bur. Amer. Ethn., pp. 43, 44, Washington, 1931.

TABULATED ANALYSIS OF 1,343 CHIPPEWA, SIOUX, UTE, MANDAN, HIDATSA, PAPAGO, PAWNEE, MENOMINEE, YUMAN, AND YAQUI SONGS

MELODIC ANALYSIS

TABLE 1.—TONALITY

	Chippewa, Sioux, Ute, Mandan, Hidatsa, Papago, Pawnee, and Menominee		Yuman and Yaqui		Total	
	Number	Per cent	Number	Per cent	Number	Per cent
Major tonality	646	53	62	49	708	53
Minor tonality	487	40	55	52	542	40
Both major and minor	8	------	1	------	9	------
Third lacking	49	4	5	3	54	3
Irregular [1]	23	2	7	5	30	4
Total	1, 213	------	130	------	1, 343	------

[1] Songs thus classified are "pure melody without tonality." In such songs the tones appear to be arranged with reference to intervals rather than with reference to a keynote.

TABLE 2.—FIRST NOTE OF SONG—ITS RELATION TO KEYNOTE

	Chippewa, Sioux, Ute, Mandan, Hidatsa, Papago, Pawnee, and Menominee		Yuman and Yaqui		Total	
	Number	Per cent	Number	Per cent	Number	Per cent
Beginning on the—						
Thirteenth	6	------	------	------	6	------
Twelfth	161	10	------	------	161	12
Eleventh	18	1	------	------	18	1
Tenth	71	6	------	------	71	5
Ninth	63	5	------	------	63	5
Octave	229	19	------	------	229	17
Seventh	20	2	------	------	20	1
Sixth	40	3	5	4	45	3
Fifth	328	28	28	21	356	27
Fourth	20	2	6	4	26	2
Third	93	8	38	30	131	12
Second	26	2	3	2	29	2
Keynote	115	9	43	33	158	11
Irregular	23	2	7	5	30	2
Total	1, 213	------	130	------	1, 343	------

TABLE 3.—LAST NOTE OF SONG—ITS RELATION TO KEYNOTE

	Chippewa, Sioux, Ute, Mandan, Hidatsa, Papago, Pawnee, and Menominee		Yuman and Yaqui		Total	
	Number	Per cent	Number	Per cent	Number	Per cent
Ending on the—						
Sixth	1	------	------	------	1	------
Fifth	408	*34*	23	*18*	431	*32*
Third	119	*10*	32	*25*	151	*11*
Second	------	------	1	------	1	------
Keynote	662	*54*	67	*50*	729	*54*
Irregular	23	*2*	7	*5*	30	*2*
Total	1, 213	------	130	------	1, 343	------

TABLE 4.—LAST NOTE OF SONG—ITS RELATION TO COMPASS

	Chippewa, Sioux, Ute, Mandan, Hidatsa, Papago, Pawnee, and Menominee		Yuman and Yaqui		Total	
	Number	Per cent	Number	Per cent	Number	Per cent
Songs in which final note is—						
Lowest in song	921	*76*	39	*30*	960	*72*
Highest in song	1	------	------	------	1	------
Immediately preceded by—						
Fifth below	1	------	------	------	1	------
Fourth below	30	*3*	8	*6*	38	*3*
Major third below	7	------	11	*8*	18	*1*
Minor third below	31	*3*	44	*34*	75	*6*
Whole tone below	22	*2*	5	*4*	27	*2*
Semitone below	10	------	5	*4*	15	*1*
Songs containing tones lower than final tone	190	*15*	18	*14*	208	*15*
Total	1, 213	------	130	------	1, 343	------

TABLE 5.—NUMBER OF TONES COMPRISED IN COMPASS OF SONG

	Chippewa, Sioux, Ute, Mandan, Hidatsa, Papago, Pawnee, and Menominee		Yuman and Yaqui		Total	
	Number	Per cent	Number	Per cent	Number	Per cent
17 tones	7	------	--------	------	7	------
14 tones	16	1	--------	------	16	1
13 tones	63	5	--------	------	63	5
12 tones	209	17	--------	------	209	16
11 tones	106	8	--------	------	106	8
10 tones	138	11	1	------	139	10
9 tones	126	10	2	------	128	7
8 tones	336	28	15	10	351	26
7 tones	69	6	40	32	109	8
6 tones	66	5	22	17	88	7
5 tones	64	5	35	27	99	7
4 tones	8	------	10	7	18	1
3 tones	5	------	5	4	10	------
Total	1, 213	------	130	------	1, 343	------

TABLE 6.—TONE MATERIAL

	Chippewa, Sioux, Ute, Mandan, Hidatsa, Papago, Pawnee, and Menominee		Yuman and Yaqui		Total	
	Number	Per cent	Number	Per cent	Number	Per cent
First 5-toned scale	20	2	--------	------	20	1
Second 5-toned scale	109	8	9	7	118	9
Fourth 5-toned scale	279	23	20	15	299	22
Fifth 5-toned scale	2	------	--------	------	2	------
Major triad	14	1	3	2	17	1
Major triad and 1 other tone	129	10	8	7	137	10
Minor triad	6	------	--------	------	6	------
Minor triad and 1 other tone	103	9	17	10	120	9
Octave complete	74	6	1	------	75	6
Octave complete except seventh	118	9	7	4	125	9
Octave complete except seventh and 1 lower tone	114	9	20	15	134	10
Octave complete except sixth	43	3	4	3	47	4
Octave complete except sixth and 1 lower tone	20	2	3	2	23	2
Octave complete except fifth and 1 lower tone	1	------	--------	------	1	------

TABLE 6.—TONE MATERIAL—Continued

	Chippewa, Sioux, Ute, Mandan, Hidatsa, Papago, Pawnee, and Menominee		Yuman and Yaqui		Total	
	Number	Per cent	Number	Per cent	Number	Per cent
Octave complete except fourth	40	*3*	2	*1*	42	*3*
Octave complete except fourth and 1 lower tone	11	------	------	------	11	------
Octave complete except third	5	------	2	*1*	7	------
Octave complete except second	29	*2*	5	*3*	34	*2*
Other combinations of tone, including irregular in tonality	96	*8*	29	*22*	125	*9*
Total	1, 213	------	130	------	1, 343	------

TABLE 7.—ACCIDENTALS

	Chippewa, Sioux, Ute, Mandan, Hidatsa, Papago, Pawnee, and Menominee		Yuman and Yaqui		Total	
	Number	Per cent	Number	Per cent	Number	Per cent
Song containing—						
No accidentals	1, 017	*83*	104	*79*	1, 121	*83*
Seventh raised a semitone	25	*2*	2	------	27	*2*
Sixth raised a semitone	18	*1*	2	*1*	20	*1*
Fourth raised a semitone	25	*2*	3	*2*	28	*2*
Third raised a semitone	4	------	------	------	4	------
Seventh lowered a semitone	1	------	4	*3*	5	------
Sixth lowered a semitone	1	------	6	------	7	------
Third lowered a semitone	4	------	------	------	4	------
Other combinations of tones including irregular in tonality	118	*10*	9	------	127	*10*
Total	1, 213	------	130	------	1, 343	------

TABLE 8.—STRUCTURE

	Chippewa, Sioux, Ute, Mandan, Hidatsa, Papago, Pawnee, and Menominee		Yuman and Yaqui		Total	
	Number	Per cent	Number	Per cent	Number	Per cent
Melodic_____	750	62	93	72	843	63
Melodic with harmonic framework_____	222	18	15	10	237	18
Harmonic_____	218	18	15	10	233	17
Irregular_____	23	2	7	5	30	2
Total_____	1, 213	_____	130	_____	1, 343	_____

TABLE 9.—FIRST PROGRESSION—DOWNWARD AND UPWARD

	Chippewa, Sioux, Ute, Mandan, Hidatsa, Papago, Pawnee, and Menominee		Yuman and Yaqui		Total	
	Number	Per cent	Number	Per cent	Number	Per cent
Downward_____	766	63	53	40	819	60
Upward_____	447	37	77	60	524	40
Total_____	1, 213	_____	130	_____	1, 343	_____

TABLE 10.—TOTAL NUMBER OF PROGRESSIONS—DOWNWARD AND UPWARD

	Chippewa, Sioux, Ute, Mandan, Hidatsa, Papago, Pawnee, and Menominee		Yuman and Yaqui		Total	
	Number	Per cent	Number	Per cent	Number	Per cent
Downward_____	20, 331	63	3, 215	53	23, 546	62
Upward_____	11, 820	37	2, 877	47	14, 697	38
Total_____	32, 151	_____	6, 092	_____	38, 243	_____

TABLE 11.—INTERVALS IN DOWNWARD PROGRESSION

	Chippewa, Sioux, Ute, Mandan, Hidatsa, Papago, Pawnee, and Menominee		Yuman and Yaqui		Total	
	Number	Per cent	Number	Per cent	Number	Per cent
Interval of a—						
Twelfth, ninth, and octave	6	------	--------	------	6	------
Seventh	6	------	--------	------	6	------
Major sixth	17	------	--------	------	17	------
Minor sixth	30	------	3	------	33	1
Fifth	168	1	34	1	202	------
Fourth	2, 111	10	292	9	2, 403	10
Major third	1, 895	9	349	10	2, 244	9
Minor third	5, 982	29	905	30	6, 887	29
Augmented second	8	------	--------	------	8	------
Major second	9, 274	46	1, 455	44	10, 729	46
Minor second	834	4	177	5	1, 011	4
Total	20, 331	------	3, 215	------	23, 546	------

TABLE 12.—INTERVALS IN UPWARD PROGRESSION

	Chippewa, Sioux, Ute, Mandan, Hidatsa, Papago, Pawnee, and Menominee		Yuman and Yaqui		Total	
	Number	Per cent	Number	Per cent	Number	Per cent
Interval of a—						
Fourteenth, twelfth, eleventh, tenth, and ninth	58	1	--------	------	58	------
Octave	162	------	4	------	166	1
Seventh	52	------	3	------	55	------
Major sixth	147	1	6	------	153	1
Minor sixth	107	------	1	------	108	------
Fifth	797	7	158	6	955	7
Fourth	2, 006	17	263	9	2, 269	15
Major third	1, 202	11	333	12	1, 535	10
Minor third	2, 832	24	830	3	3, 662	24
Major second	4, 009	34	1, 123	40	5, 132	35
Minor second	448	4	156	6	604	4
Total	11, 820	------	2, 877	------	14, 697	------

TABLE 13.—AVERAGE NUMBER OF SEMITONES IN AN INTERVAL

	Chippewa, Sioux, Ute, Mandan, Hidatsa, Papago, Pawnee, and Menominee		Yuman and Yaqui		Total	
	Number	Per cent	Number	Per cent	Number	Per cent
Number of songs_____	1, 213	_____	130	_____	1, 343	_____
Number of intervals_____	32, 151	_____	6, 092	_____	38, 243	_____
Number of semitones_____	98, 863	_____	17, 697	_____	116, 560	_____
Average number of semitones in an interval_____	3. 07	_____	2. 9	_____	3. 03	_____

RHYTHMIC ANALYSIS

TABLE 14.—PART OF MEASURE ON WHICH SONG BEGINS

	Chippewa, Sioux, Ute, Mandan, Hidatsa, Papago, Pawnee, and Menominee		Yuman and Yaqui		Total	
	Number	Per cent	Number	Per cent	Number	Per cent
Beginning on unaccented part of measure_____	472	*38*	68	*51*	540	*40*
Beginning on accented part of measure_____	698	*58*	62	*49*	760	*56*
Transcribed in outline_____	42	*3*	_____	_____	42	3
Without measure accents_____	1	_____	_____	_____	1	_____
Total_____	1, 213	_____	130	_____	1, 343	_____

TABLE 15.—RHYTHM (METER) OF FIRST MEASURE

	Chippewa, Sioux, Ute, Mandan, Hidatsa, Papago, Pawnee, and Me-nominee		Yuman and Yaqui		Total	
	Number	Per cent	Number	Per cent	Number	Per cent
First measure in—						
2–4 time_____	682	56	93	71	775	57
3–4 time_____	426	35	28	20	454	34
4–4 time_____	9	_____	_____	_____	9	_____
5–4 time_____	16	1	1	_____	17	1
6–4 time_____	1	_____	_____	_____	1	_____
7–4 time_____	2	_____	_____	_____	2	_____
3–8 time_____	11	_____	3	2	14	1
4–8 time_____	6	_____	1	_____	7	_____
5–8 time_____	12	1	2	1	14	1
6–8 time_____	1	_____	1	_____	2	_____
7–8 time_____	1	_____	1	_____	2	_____
2–2 time_____	3	_____	_____	_____	3	_____
Transcribed in outline_____	42	3	_____	_____	42	3
Without measure accents_____	1	_____	_____	_____	1	_____
Total_____	1, 213	_____	130	_____	1, 343	_____

TABLE 16.—CHANGE OF TIME (MEASURE LENGTHS)

	Chippewa, Sioux, Ute, Mandan, Hidatsa, Papago, Pawnee, and Me-nominee		Yuman and Yaqui		Total	
	Number	Per cent	Number	Per cent	Number	Per cent
Songs containing no change of time_____	182	15	34	26	216	16
Songs containing a change of time_____	988	81	96	74	1, 084	80
Transcribed in outline_____	42	3	_____	_____	42	3
Without measure accents_____	1	_____	_____	_____	1	_____
Total_____	1, 213	_____	130	_____	1, 343	_____

TABLE 17.—RHYTHMIC UNIT

	Chippewa, Sioux, Ute, Mandan, Hidatsa, Papago, Pawnee, and Menominee		Yuman and Yaqui		Total	
	Number	Per cent	Number	Per cent	Number	Per cent
Songs containing—						
No rhythmic unit_____	335	28	44	34	379	28
1 rhythmic unit_____	665	55	60	46	725	54
2 rhythmic units_____	142	10	21	16	163	12
3 rhythmic units_____	22	1	3	1	25	2
4 rhythmic units_____	5	------	2	1	7	------
5 rhythmic units_____	2	------	------	------	2	------
Transcribed in outline_____	42	3	------	------	42	3
Total_____	1,213	------	130	------	1,343	------

DESCRIPTIVE ANALYSIS

The purpose of this analysis and the accompanying tables is to show the simplest characteristics of the songs and to afford opportunity for a comparison between the various tribes under observation. After establishing the resemblances in a sufficiently large number of songs a table of analysis is discontinued. Five such tables, used in earlier work, are not used at the present time. These comprised tables showing the tempo (metric unit) of voice and drum, and a table comparing these tempi, a table showing the key of the songs, and a table showing the rhythm of the accompanying instrument. The first three were last used in the analysis of 710 songs (Bull. 75, Tables 20, 21, 22 on pp. 48, 49, 50, 51), and the fourth was last used in the comparative analysis of 820 songs (Bull. 80, p. 26). In the first of these tables the highest percentage in the tempo of the voice varied from 76 to 96, according to the metronome, 36 per cent being between these numbers, with the highest (7 per cent) in the number of songs having 92 as their tempo. The highest percentages in the tempo of the drum, rattle, or morache were between 92 and 120, 58 per cent of the songs being in this group, with the highest (10 per cent) having 104 as their tempo. This indicated the general tempi of the songs. Another table showed the voice to be in the same tempo as the accompaniment in 51 per cent, faster in 16 per cent, and slower in 32 per cent of the songs recorded with drum or other instrument. This showed that the Indian is able to maintain two distinct tempi at the same time, and the basis of analysis was discontinued.

The analysis of 710 songs according to key showed the highest percentages occurring between F and B, the highest within the group having 8 per cent in the key of G major, and the next having 6 per cent in the key of F major. In determining this pitch the phonograph was played at the same speed as when the record was made and compared with a piano tuned to standard pitch (A, 440 vibrations). The table was then discontinued.

The classification of the accompaniment rhythm was continued during the study of Mandan and Hidatsa music, the total number of songs then under analysis being 820. (Bull. 80, Table 18 on pp. 25, 26.) In 61 per cent of the songs recorded with accompaniment the drum, rattle, or morache was in strokes of equal force, each approximately equivalent to an eighth, quarter, or half note of the melody. In 33 per cent the stroke was either preceded or followed by a short unaccented stroke and in 5 per cent the accompaniment was in strokes that were equally spaced, with an accent on alternate strokes. This group is classified as "eighth notes accented in groups of two." From these analyses it appears evident that an even pulse of the accompaniment was preferred by the Indians under observation, though the tempo might not correspond to that of the voice. This basis of cumulative analysis was then discontinued. The Papago sing with rattle and basket drum, and their songs were not analyzed in this respect. The accompaniment rhythms of the Pawnee were analyzed, and confirm the findings in 820 songs previously analyzed. (Bull. 93, Table 18, p. 125.) A general observation of the Menominee songs showed the same characteristic. The present group, however, contains a wide variety in accompaniment rhythms. This is shown in the group analysis (Table 18, p. 207), but the comparative table is not resumed.

The foregoing data are presented in order that the student may carry forward the comparison, if desired, by observing these peculiarities in the present group of songs. These tables are intended to assist the understanding of Indian songs by simple standards applicable to large series. They should not be understood as an attempt at exhaustive analyses. Familiar terminology and bases of classification are adopted as conducive to the purpose of the system.

Attention is here directed to comparisons made in the consideration of Yuman and Yaqui songs which supplement the present comparative analysis. (See pp. 19–23.)

TABLE 1.—The Yuman and Yaqui resemble the Papago in having less than half their songs in major tonality and a considerable percentage in somewhat irregular groups.

This suggests that "key" in the musician's use of that term is found to a lesser degree in recorded Papago, Yuman, and Yaqui songs than in the songs of tribes previously analyzed. In this connection it is interesting to note that the Yuman and Yaqui tribes are distinct from the Papago in general culture, and that the resemblance here noted would be difficult to detect in listening to the songs.

Several factors are taken into consideration in designating the keynote of a song for the purpose of analysis. No theory is advanced that the keynote is part of a musical system, consciously followed by the singer. It is simply a "point of repose" in the melodic progressions. The tone is decided upon by the test of the ear, and by the relations of the tones in melodic sequence. Thus if a song contained only the tones C, E, and G, the tone C would be regarded as the keynote if it were the most prominent, accented tone. If C occurred only as an unaccented, passing tone, and E were the most prominent tone the song might conceivably be analyzed in the key of E minor, or possibly as irregular in tonality. In a majority of instances the keynote is not difficult to determine if one admits the test of a musician's ear; in some instances it is debatable by any standard, and in others it is so uncertain that the songs are classified for the present as "irregular in tonality."

A small number of songs are sung four times and then ended at any desired point (see pp. 18, 42).

TABLE 2.—The foregoing resemblance to the Papago and difference from tribes previously analyzed is shown in the classification of the first and last notes. In the Yuman and Yaqui songs 33 per cent begin on the keynote, 30 per cent on its third, and 21 per cent on its fifth, none of the songs having a compass of an octave. In the Papago songs 24 per cent began on the keynote and 6 per cent on its octave, a few Papago songs having this larger compass. In the 1,213 songs previously analyzed only 9 per cent began on the keynote, but 19 per cent began on its octave, these songs having a much larger compass than the songs recorded on the Mexican border.

TABLE 3.—A strange contrast to all tribes previously analyzed is shown in the relative proportion of songs ending on the third and fifth above the keynote, this being the only group with the larger percentage on the third. The percentage ending on the keynote is smaller than in the total number of songs previously analyzed. This is a peculiarity of this group of Indians and no explanation is suggested.

TABLE 4.—A large number of Yuman and Yaqui songs lie partly above and partly below the keynote. It will be noted that the final tone is the lowest in only 30 per cent of these songs, in contrast to 76 per cent in the songs previously analyzed. The trend of the melody is shown by the fact that in 34 per cent of the songs the final tone is immediately preceded by a minor third lower, and in 8 per cent it is preceded by a major third lower.

TABLE 5.—Only two songs of this group have a compass of more than eight tones, while in the songs previously analyzed 52 per cent had a compass of more than an octave. The largest group of Yuman and Yaqui songs has a compass of seven tones and comprises 32 per cent of the entire number, the next in size being the songs with a compass of five tones comprising 27 per cent. In songs previously analyzed these groups have comprised respectively 6 and 5 per cent of the total.

TABLE 6.—The percentage of songs on the familiar major and minor pentatonic scales is considerably less in this than in the total number of songs previously analyzed, comprising 22 per cent in this and 33 per cent in the former songs. Higher percentages appear in the songs containing the minor triad and one other tone, and the octave complete except for the seventh and one lower tone. The songs based on the major triad and one other tone are less than in the songs previously analyzed, though there is a higher percentage of songs containing only the major triad.

TABLE 7.—Accidentals, or tones diatonically altered, appear in a larger percentage of Yuman and Yaqui than of songs previously analyzed, an especially interesting group being the four songs with seventh lowered a semitone, three of which are major in tonality.

TABLE 8.—In structure the Yuman and Yaqui songs are more freely melodic than any songs previously analyzed. This is in accord with the results shown in the other tables of analysis.

TABLES 9 AND 10.—A distinctive peculiarity of these songs appears in these tables, the percentage of songs beginning with an upward progression being larger than in any other tribe under analysis and the percentage of upward progressions being larger than in the other tribes.

TABLES 11 AND 12.—The percentages of various intervals in downward progression resemble those of other analyzed tribes, these percentages being more nearly alike than in a majority of the tables, but the ascending progressions show interesting differences. The minor third, which has occurred in other tribes so frequently as to constitute 24 per cent of the total intervals, is found to comprise only 3 per cent of the intervals in Yuman and Yaqui songs, while the whole tone, constituting 34 per cent of the preceding group, comprises 40 per cent in the Yuman and Yaqui songs. The semitone is also more frequent in occurrence. The vigorous interval of an ascending fourth shows about half its percentages in the songs previously analyzed. Thus we see that the Yuman and Yaqui songs progress upward by smaller and different intervals and a larger variety of intervals than songs of other tribes, but progress downward by practically the same intervals.

TABLE 13.—The average number of semitones in an interval is smaller than in any former group except the old Sioux songs in which the average was 2.89. In the comparatively modern Sioux songs the average was 2.97. By this analysis it appears that the general trend of Yuman and Yaqui melody is by smaller intervals than in any other recorded tribe except the Sioux.

TABLE 14.—Songs of directness and action have been found to begin generally with an accented tone. In the Yuman and Yaqui only 49 per cent have this beginning, 51 per cent beginning on the unaccented portion of the measure. In songs previously analyzed 58 per cent begin on the accented and 38 on the unaccented parts of a measure, the remaining 4 per cent being transcribed in outline or without measure accents.

TABLE 15.—The gentle smoothness of Yuman and Yaqui songs appears also in the rhythm of their opening measures, 71 per cent beginning in double time, contrasted with 56 per cent in songs previously analyzed. The percentage of songs beginning in 3–4, 3–8, and 5–8 time is smaller than in other recorded tribes.

TABLE 16.—The smooth flow of Yuman and Yaqui songs is further shown in this table, 26 per cent of these songs containing no change of measure length while only 15 per cent of songs previously analyzed were without this irregularity of rhythm.

TABLE 17.—The percentages in this table are consistent with those in previous tables, 34 per cent of these songs containing no rhythmic unit, in contrast to 28 per cent in the songs previously analyzed. The songs containing one rhythmic unit are proportionately less than in other songs but the songs containing two rhythmic units are more than in the other tribes, comprising 16 per cent instead of 10 per cent. Reference to the tribal analysis on page 207 and a comparison of the serial numbers with the list of songs shows that six of the songs with two rhythmic units are concerning birds and animals, one is concerning the hunt, two are modern Yaqui songs, and the remainder are songs of dances, apparently held for pleasure. These are the sources of the most rhythmic songs of the tribes under observation, the smaller percentages reflecting the characteristics of the long cycles of songs.

The rhythmic element of Yuman and Yaqui music is contained in the accompaniment rather than in the songs. These rhythms are shown in Table 18, page 207, which is not carried forward in the total analysis. Six different rhythms occurred in the accompaniment of more than one song, and various interrupted rhythms are transcribed with the melodies.

CREMATION

It is the belief of the Yuma, Cocopa, and Mohave that if a man's body is not cremated his spirit will "wander around and talk to its relatives in their dreams." The origin of this ancient custom is contained in traditions and series of songs which are similar in these tribes.[17] Cremation usually takes place less than 24 hours after death. In former times a body was cremated in or near the dwelling of the family, but in 1912 the superintendent of the Yuma Reservation, Mr. L. L. Odle, persuaded the people to have all the cremations in one place, setting aside a tract of ground not far from the agency. After about 300 bodies had been cremated at this place it became advisable to select another, and a similar plat was assigned to the purpose a little nearer the agency. Both places were visited by the writer, and in neither place was there any evidence that the surface of the ground had been disturbed. The present plat (1922) is about a quarter of a mile from the foot of the hill on which the agency is located, and comprises about 2 or 3 acres. At one end of this tract of land the bodies are cremated and at the other end is a space for the teams and horses of those who attend the cremations. In the middle of the space is a log house and near it is a " desert shelter," consisting of the usual thatched roof supported by logs. Under this is an old spring bed, raised from the ground by corner posts about a foot high. On this bed the body is laid before its cremation, being brought thither immediately after death occurs. The Yuma believe that the spirit remains in the body until cremation, when it departs. All the personal belongings of the deceased are burned, except the garments needed for clothing the image if he is to be "honored " in the Károk or Memorial ceremony. Animals were formerly sacrificed and money is still thrown into the fire, but the articles burned at the present time consist chiefly of clothing. Persons who have suffered the loss of friends throw articles of clothing or other valuables into the flames, believing that the spirit in its departure will carry these articles to the spirits of their friends. An informant said: " We can replace the clothing. It is a greater honor to give to the dead than to hang on to our personal belongings."

The Yuma do not believe, however, that the spirit of the dead goes at once to the spirit land. It is said to be too inexperienced and unaccustomed to its changed condition to travel at once, so it lingers four days near the place where it has lived. Then it can " see its way " and it goes to the wind quarters and then to the abode of the spirits.

---

[17] Cf. Putnam, A Yuma Cremation, Amer. Anth., Vol. VIII, pp. 264–267.

There is a difference in the form of cremation for chiefs and for unimportant members of the tribe. At the cremation of chiefs or prominent persons there is a certain ceremonial procedure, the songs of the origin legend are sung, and a very old rattle is used by the man in charge of the event. Frank Pasquale was a leader of the cremation and Kârok in the early days, and Charles Wilson and Chief Miguel sang with him as helpers, learning the songs in that manner. Miguel is dead and Wilson no longer takes an active part in the ceremonies, the songs being sung by his son, Joe Homer, who is blind, and his nephew, Bill Wilson. The songs, however, are understood to be the property of Charles Wilson.

A set of cremation songs may contain only two or three songs, though the usual number is four. There are four sets of songs to each half of the night, and four verses to each song. A peculiarity of the Kârok songs is that they are sung through four times and then ended at any point in the melody. A further peculiarity is that the singing ends on a low tone which is prolonged in a nasal, humming sound.

The rattle used at a cremation ceremony consists of a string of dewclaws forming a loop which is held in the hand. Formerly it was kept by George Chino, a prominent member of the tribe, who received it from his grandfather. At present Joe Homer keeps this rattle and used it in the ceremony witnessed by the writer. The tradition concerning this rattle is as follows: In old times the Yuma came down from the north. On the journey they were hungry and a deer rushed out of the wilderness. The chief gathered his braves together and said, "Anyone who can get the deer will be honored." He sent out four men, one after another. The fourth man overtook the deer on the run. He came alongside the deer and had a sharp instrument with which he " hamstrung " the animal so that it fell. This saved the tribe from starvation.[18] A rattle was made of the four dewclaws from this deer and they are supposed to be in the rattle used at the present time. As long as the people could get dewclaws, they added one for each cremation. This continued until there were about 200. In recent years it has been impossible to get these dewclaws, except that a few were brought from the north and added in honor of Frank Pasquale, a chief who died a few years ago. The rattle is now so old that some of the claws are loose.

The duration of a cremation ceremony depends upon circumstances as well as upon the prominence of the person for whom it is held. An interesting example of this took place in 1921 in connection with the cremation of a young man named Lee Rainbow, who enlisted in the United States Army during the World War,

---

[18] This narrative is given as nearly as possible in the words of the interpreter.

went to France, and is said to have been the first Indian who died overseas.[19] He was buried in France, but his body was later brought to America and cremated on the reservation. There was ample time for preparation, and the people sang every Saturday and Sunday for several weeks and almost continuously for a week before the cremation. The informant said he remembered that the songs of the Human Being dance, the Mohave bird songs, and the Yuman bird songs were sung before Rainbow's cremation; also the cycles of the Sun, the Frog, and the Raven, as well as Rainbow's personal songs. Games were played at night. Sometimes three or four groups were singing at the same time, in the same house, each singing a different song. The latter was not done in the old days.

THE CREMATION OF BERNARD FLAME

An opportunity for witnessing this rite of the Yuma occurred on February 13, 1922, the writer being present at the cremation of Bernard Flame. The ceremony was given as it would have been given for a chief, because Bernard Flame had been a singer at cremations, singing with Joe Homer, Bill Wilson, and Miguel, who were leaders of the ceremony. He had an understanding with Homer that whichever survived, the other should sing at his cremation a certain song beginning with the words, " The tomahawk says." These words are in the " old language " and a translation could not be obtained. The promise was fulfilled at the cremation. A further claim to honor was the man's Yuma name and the manner in which he received it. His Yuma name was Atcpa'mkivam, meaning " captured ball." This name was given him when he won in a game resembling shinny except that the ball was buried in the ground about 1½ inches before the game began. This was a difficult game and the victor was accorded high honors. The name was explained as follows: The stick used in playing the game was called tcata's; the ball, about 1 inch in diameter, was called i'tcatas, and after the ball had been brought out of the hole it was called a'tcapam, meaning " out of the hole." Four men played the game, two playing as partners. At first the four men stood around the hole in which the ball had been placed and tried to raise it with their sticks. When the ball had been brought to the surface of the ground the successful man and his partner were obliged to defend it against their opponents, all using their sticks. Retaining the ball constituted a victory and the captured (retained) ball was called acpa'mkivam.

---

[19] The father of this young man, Nelson Rainbow by name, acted as one of the interpreters during the writer's work among the Cocopa, translating that language into Yuma, while Luke Homer, the Yuman interpreter, translated it into English. Rainbow also recorded two songs of the peon game (Nos. 124, 125).

Bernard Flame died in a sanatorium for the insane, where he had been confined for seven years. When he began to act strangely there was an effort to trace his condition to the action of some medicine man, and "it made a great deal of trouble among the people." Later he was sent to the sanatorium. His condition was not believed to change his personality any more than an ordinary illness would have done.

The body arrived at Yuma by train on the evening of February 12, and the wailing began at once. It was not unusual for wailing to begin before death actually occurred. This wailing comprises every audible expression of passionate grief and is heart-rending to hear. That evening it was decided that they would sing four times during the night and four times while the body lay in state the next morning. The father of the dead man made four speeches, one when the body arrived, another before and another after midnight, and a fourth at sunrise. In the first he talked of the infancy and childhood of the deceased, in the second and third he told of his boyhood and early manhood, and in the fourth speech he told of his son's mature life. It is the custom, when making these speeches for a man about 40 years old, to divide his life into periods of about 10 years each, the speeches summarizing the events of his life according to those periods. On the day of the cremation four ceremonial speeches were made by the leaders of the ceremony, chief of whom was Joe Homer. (See p. 46.) One speech was made while the body lay in state, the second and third were in praise of his life and expressed sympathy for his family, and the fourth was made at the place of cremation after the fire was lighted. This speech completed the man's history, told what he did to benefit the tribe, and was said to "take the man on his way to the spirit land." These speeches were in the "old language." The following sentences were said to be part of the final speech, but their connection is uncertain: "If you happen to take the right road as I have done, you may at my age talk the language I have received from the old men." "Open the way for him so that he can travel right and enter the happy hunting ground." Joe Homer allowed a Cocopa to make this speech.

The writer went to the cremation ground February 13 at about 11 o'clock in the morning. The body was lying on the spring cot under the shelter or shack, closely surrounded by relatives and friends. They sat on the cot close to the body and frequently took up the hands and fondled them as they wept. Others sat on the ground, often resting their head and arms on the body and wailing. Behind them the people stood in a compact crowd. The father of the dead man sat on the ground at the foot of the cot in extreme grief. The crowd separated and allowed the writer to approach this primitive bier and see the body, which was dressed as usual except that a handkerchief was tied over the face with a corner hanging loosely above the chin. A handkerchief was tied over the hair and knotted above the forehead, according to the Yuma custom. A pack of cards was on the chest and a red blanket was under the body. Tears were shed profusely by men and women, especially the men, both young and old. There was much sobbing but not as much " artificial wailing " as in the afternoon, when shrill cries, high and penetrating, were heard. The writer shook hands with the people and distributed cigarettes. No preparations for the cremation could be seen at that time.

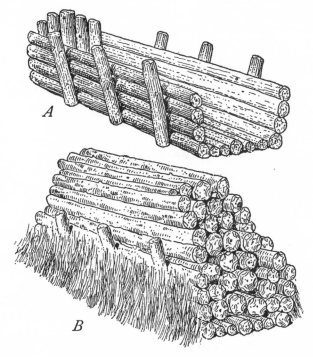

FIGURE 3.—Cremation crib (a) and pyre (b)

At about 1 o'clock she returned and found a larger assemblage than in the morning. One hundred persons were standing around the body, facing toward it, and it seemed as though everyone were making a noise. On approaching the place it was seen that the mourners were becoming exhausted, and during the next hour the shrill cries of the less personally interested men and women were the more in evidence.

The place for the burning of the body had been prepared and was located perhaps 250 or 300 feet from the shelter. A shallow trench had been dug and the earth placed carefully at one side. This earth was about two bushels in quantity, showing that the trench was not deep. Above this a frame or crib was constructed of cottonwood logs which had been concealed in the brush, so that the making of the frame required only a short time. This frame was more than 10 feet long and consisted of a floor of logs sloping slightly toward the foot and to one side. Upright logs about 4 feet high were at the head and horizontal logs to the same height at the sides, secured by wire to upright posts. These were farther apart at the top than next the floor of the structure. Outside were small branches of arrow weed, placed upright on the ground, slanting against the logs. (Fig. 4.) A short distance from this structure were piled the additional logs that would be placed above the body.

The ceremony began in the shelter where the body lay in state. Joe Homer and Bill Wilson took their places at the head of the body, Homer holding the dewclaw rattle. Chief Miguel, who formerly shared this responsibility, had died a few years prior to this event. The manner of shaking the rattle at this time was "the highest honor and done only for a chief or man of equal importance." Standing back of the dead man, Homer lowered the rattle toward his face with a trembling motion, raised it slowly with a gentle shaking, and then brought it sharply downward with a motion like a blow. This was done toward each point of the compass beginning with the north, though Homer did not change his position. (It will be recalled that the spirit of the dead goes to the four windquarters before going to the spirit land.) There was a pause between the repetitions, and one of the ceremonial speeches was made at this time. The body was then lifted on a blanket and the procession started toward the crib, led by Homer and Bill Wilson. All the company followed in this procession.

Two stops or pauses were made on the way, one of these being ceremonial and the other for some arrangement of details. The body was laid on the ground near the crib. Fully 200 persons were present, standing close together in the compact crowding which was noted in the morning. Then followed an encircling of the crib, which was a great honor and usually reserved for those who were to be honored in the Kârok or Memorial ceremony the next summer. This circling began at the south, or foot of the crib, then moving to the east, north, and west, the group moving outside the body as it lay near the foot of the open crib. Four women walked backward, each waving a bundle of " presents " consisting of clothing, and four men walked forward, one being Homer, who continued to shake the rattle. At this time they sang the second of two songs that had been sung under the "shelter." A pause was made at each of the cardinal points where songs were sung that mentioned the wind quarters. The rhythm was marked by stamping the feet, and the action was the same as in a dance at the Kârok and in the Deer dance. When a dancer stamped his right foot he allowed his right hand to hang below his knee, putting his left hand and arm behind him. This was reversed when he stamped the other foot.

The wailing continued, one man sobbing as though physically exhausted. It was learned that they were waiting for a woman who was expected from a distant village, and at last she appeared, walking with a stout cane and repeating a high, shrill cry from time to time as she crossed the cremation ground, her cotton mantle blown backward by the motion of her walking. When she arrived the body was lifted on the blanket and laid on the log floor of the framework, the blanket being drawn smoothly over it and the man's personal belongings placed beside him. The body was laid face downward, as it is the belief that if it is laid in any other position the spirit will " wander around." After it was in position the men in charge of this portion of the event brought the additional logs and laid them above the body, extending the length of the structure. Many of these logs were slightly bent mid length, making a knee which was placed uppermost and protected the body from pressure. Songs were sung with the gourd rattle, one of these songs promising the dead man that he would be honored in the Kàrok, in the next summer. Cottonwood logs were piled higher than the top of the horizontal sides of the crib. The casket in which the body had been shipped was taken from its box and placed on top of the logs and on it were placed gifts of clothing, handkerchiefs, and other articles. The shipping box was then placed on top of the pyre beside the coffin. A man who carried a flaming bundle of branches then lit the arrow-weed stalks around the pyre, lighting them close to the ground in several places. The flames rose quickly, the logs being very dry. There was much crackling but little smoke, the pyre being enveloped in a solid mass of flame. Women tore off their dresses and threw them into the fire. Some of these were silk dresses, having the full, long skirt worn by the Yuma women, with much trimming of white lace. A good winter coat was among the garments thrown into the fire. During the first few minutes a young woman, waving her arms rhythmically, rushed near the flames as if in great grief.

Within 10 minutes after the lighting of the fire the people were hitching up their teams to go away, and by the time the fire was out only the mourners remained. This is the custom, leaving the family alone as soon as possible. The ashes fell into the shallow trench, and the earth, which had been placed conveniently near, was quickly replaced, the ground was smoothed over, and all traces of the cremation obliterated. The writer visited the place about two hours after a former cremation had taken place and the only persons to be seen were three or four women, sitting with bowed heads. No trace of the cremation was visible, but undoubtedly they were sitting around the spot where the fire had burned.

The mourners and singers must fast four days after a cremation, eating as little as possible and avoiding salt and lard. There is no " funeral feast " as among some tribes, either before or after the rite, and no food, tobacco, or cooking utensils are placed with the dead.

The name of the dead is not spoken until the Kårok, after which it is unspoken forever; neither is the dead referred to in any manner.

A Cremation Incident

The following incident was related: A young woman suffered from chronic dysentery and death was believed to occur. Preparations were at once begun for her cremation, but she came to life and later was able to tell her experiences. She was supposed to have died late in the afternoon. All that night she believed herself in a thicket of arrow weeds, without clothing. She could hear the crying, and distinguished the voice of her mother, and she could see her own body lying in the center of the open " shack." Whenever she looked up she saw people passing her hiding place, and heard them refer to her by terms of relationship. They were on their way to her cremation. She stood there feeling sorry for her mother and not knowing what to do. Toward morning, after they had moved her body to another shack, she ran over to another thicket and another until she came close to the " crib " or cremation frame. The logs were green and the place looked like a shelter from the sun. She went in and sat in the little space, looking toward the shack where her body lay.

At last the time came when she knew they were going to move the body and cremate it. Running as hard as she could run, she went into the shack and lay down beside her own body, holding it so they could not move it. She held it close for a few moments until it began to regain consciousness. When she revived she could barely hear the people crying. Her jaws were rigidly set, her upper lip was drawn back, showing her teeth, and her tongue was thrown back. She could hardly open her eyes. She was stiff, but they held a mirror over her mouth and saw that life was returning, so they had the Indian doctors rub her body. They rubbed around her eyes and at last she opened her eyes and recognized people. She could scarcely speak at first, but by evening she could talk a little.

She lived a normal life for some time and had no return of her illness.

YUMAN LEGEND CONNECTED WITH CREMATION CUSTOM AND MEMORIAL CEREMONY

The time required for a complete narration of this legend, with the singing of the songs, is about nine hours. Two versions of the early portion of the story were recorded, one by Joe (Jose) Homer, the blind leader of the songs at cremations, and the other by Peter Hammon, a recognized authority on old songs and customs. Both versions were the subject of consultation with Charles Wilson (Pl. 1 and pp. 100–129), the father of Joe Homer, who owns the songs used in the cremation and memorial ceremony. He explained some details and made slight additions to the narratives. Both informants said the songs are always accompanied by beating on an inverted basket with bundles of slender arrow weeds, Homer stating that two men beat on the basket but only one sang the songs. The early portion of the story is presented in Homer's version.

There were once two boys who were children of a bird called wĭ'tsawĭts and also called tcowĭ'ts. It is a common bird with a yellow breast that comes in the spring. These boys were named A'xtakwa'some' and Pu'kuhan (pronounced Po'kohan by the other informant). They went out to get material for making a flute.[20] One boy took the material in his hand and said, " The girls will love me when I play this flute." This is expressed in the following song.

No. 1. "I Will Make a Flute"

(Catalogue No. 1238)

Recorded by JOE HOMER

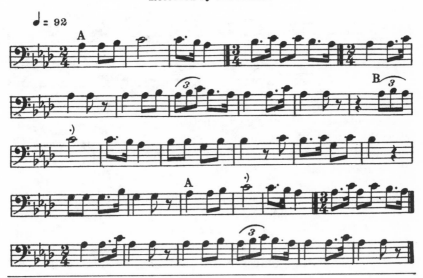

---

[20] Two other legends of the origin of the flute have been recorded by the writer, together with their melodies. Among the Mandan the first flute was said to have been made from a sunflower stalk. It had magic power, but was not a courting instrument. (Bull. 80, pp. 80–84.) Among the Papago the first flute was made of cane, and its making was connected with a story of two boys, similar to the legend here presented. (Bull. 90, pp. 54–77.)

Analysis.—This melody consists of three periods, the third being a repetition of the first. On comparing it with the melodies played on the flute, as transcribed from actual performances, we note a similarity in the ascent to a sustained tone and in the ascent and descent within two or three measures. The framework of this song consists of the major third A flat–C, with G occurring only in the second period. No rhythmic unit occurs, although the melody is strongly rhythmic in character.

When the flute was finished he played on it, and the first melody he played is said to have been that of the following song. The words of the song, continuing the thread of the narrative, were as follows: "I have the flute in my mouth. Anyone living far away will hear and come to listen."

No. 2. "I Have Finished the Flute"

(Catalogue No. 1239)

Recorded by JOE HOMER

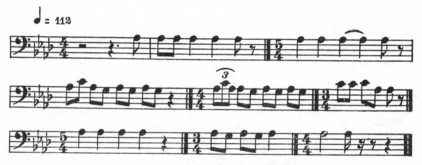

Analysis.—This is such a melody as a beginner might play on an instrument. It contains many repetitions of a single tone and has little that is interesting in either melody or rhythm. The framework is the same as in the song next preceding except for the omission of B flat.

These boys grew to manhood and each took two wives. The younger man died, and when the tribe was journeying toward the east one of his wives bore a child. The life of this child was threatened by an old blind man, father of the younger man's wives and an enemy of the flute players. This old man said that if the child were a boy he would cook and eat him, but if it were a girl he would keep her because she could help cook and bring water.[22] This portion of the narrative is contained in the words of the following song.

---

[22] According to the later informant the child's life was similarly threatened by its paternal uncle, Coyote.

No. 3. The Wonder-boy is Born

(Catalogue No. 1240)

Recorded by JOE HOMER

Analysis.—This song is characterized by an ascending major second at the close of a phrase which is unusual and seems to suggest uncertainty concerning the "Wonder-boy." The only tones occurring in the melody are F, G, A, B flat, the latter being regarded as the keynote. In this, as in numerous other songs of the Indians, a "key" in the musician's use of the term can scarcely be assumed to exist, and the signature should be understood chiefly as a means of indicating the pitch of certain tones, the designation of a keynote being tentative. The most interesting phrase is found in the fourth and fifth measures and recurs occasionally during the melody. No accompaniment was recorded, but the rattle used with the song was probably in the rhythm shown with No. 4, which conforms to the rhythm in a phrase of the present melody.

The mother of the child had as great medicine power as its enemy, so she caused the child's voice in crying to be that of a girl, though the child was a boy. This saved its life.

Both informants stated that the boy was named Mitpa'khumi; that he desired to change this name; and that he had a half brother whom he later met and recognized.

At this point the work with Homer was discontined, and the remainder of the material, both story and song, was obtained from a man known as Peter Hammon, whose Yuman name is Misàhai'kwakiu'. He is considered a particularly good singer of the old songs, and according to his custom he brought with him two bundles of arrow weed for pounding on the basket as accompaniment to the songs. He said that he inherited this series of songs and they belong to him. It takes all night for him to sing the entire series, and the people who ask him to sing the songs provide food at about midnight. As in similar instances, the singer experienced difficulty in condensing the material and selecting typical songs. The series is not complete, but the number is sufficient for present purposes. The words of the songs were summarized by the singer before the song was recorded. These songs were called Ata'xamaili' and "were not sung very loud."

The first song recorded by Hammon is concerning the Wonder-boy on his journey. He stops occasionally and thinks of the name (Mitpa'khumi) that was given him by his paternal uncle Coyote, who was called Hatpa'akwa's. He is not satisfied with his name and decides that he will select one "fitted to himself."

No. 4. The Wonder-boy Decides to Change His Name

(Catalogue No. 1213)

Recorded by PETER HAMMON

Voice ♩ = 104
Rattle ♩ = 104
See rattle-rhythm below

Rattle rhythm

Analysis.—Attention is here directed to the correspondence between the idea and the form of the song which is evident throughout this group recorded by Hammon. In this song the child is starting on his travels and is considering a change in his name. The latter is more common among Indians than among persons of the white race. The idea of the song is simple and the structure of the song is both simple and interesting. The first period begins with a 4-measure phrase and the second with a 2-measure phrase, but the closing phrase is the same. In the 5–8 measure we find the break in the time which is so often introduced midway through an Indian song, adding to its interest. The melody tones are those of the major triad and sixth, and the song has a range of six tones. In repetitions of the song each section was sometimes sung twice. The rhythm of the drum is simple and the drum and voice were synchronous.

The next song states that as he traveled along he was satisfied with a certain name and said, " This day I will be known throughout the world as Po′kohan." [23] In explanation of this name it was said that *Po* came from his ancestors and is in some way connected with Coyote, while he himself added the termination.

No. 5. The Wonder-boy Selects a New Name

(Catalogue No. 1214)

Recorded by PETER HAMMON

Voice ♩ = 112
Rattle ♩ = 112
Rattle-rhythm similar to No. 4

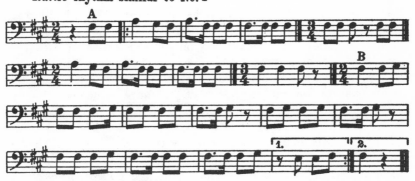

Analysis.—The assertive phrases at the opening of this song seem to express the decision of the Wonder-boy in regard to his name.

---

[23] According to another informant the boy said " Mitpa′khumi is a bad name because I have not seen my father, so I will take the name of Kwi′yahoma." The meaning of this name is not known.

They are characterized by an ascent of a minor third to an accented tone. The second period (B) contains only the tones F sharp and G sharp with continuous progression between these tones. Rests occur after four measures until the 2-measure phrase in period B which ends somewhat abruptly. The tone E occurs only in the connective measure between repetitions of the song.

As the Wonder-boy continued his journey he came to the place where he was born. He found the house deserted and nothing but tracks of birds and snakes around the place. He entered the shack and stood there with his eyes closed and his hands over his eyes. He stood there for a whole hour. Then he took his hands from his eyes and saw the garments and paraphernalia of his ancestors hanging on the wall. There were war bonnets, garments decorated with feathers, and many similar articles, and he put them on and went outdoors and admired himself. Then he changed his mind and took the things back and hung them where he had found them. He kept one small article which was made of bamboo and called axta'kasà. He said, "This was used by my ancestors to enable them to go without water for a long time. I will take it, as I shall need it on my travels." He took another article called ha'punor, saying, "I will need this also on my wanderings. It will enable me to go without food." This article was a belt to be worn around the waist. He took also a war bonnet, saying, "I will wear this to keep the sun off my head in my travels." He also took a fourth article, which was a bag, hung over his shoulder. He went out of the shack carrying these four articles.

As he traveled on and on he had in his mind only one desire, and that was to see some of his ancestors. After going quite a distance he stopped and made a fire, then he turned around and put water on it, putting it out. He piled up the hot, wet ashes, ran his hand through them, and brought up his father, who had died before the boy's birth. The features did not look like those of a human being, but the boy recognized his father. Then his father spoke and said, "I am glad to see you, my son, but you must remember that my bones, such as my shins, are being used by other people as shinny sticks, and that the man who killed me has caused me to inhale nothing but this dust so that I would become dry and could not be brought to life again."

The boy said, "All right, father. Although I have the power to bring you back to life again, I will not do it. This shall be an example throughout all future years." [24]

---

[24] If the boy had restored his father to life it would have been possible for every human being to be restored to life by medicine power.

After the boy said this he put his father back into the ashes whence he had come. This is narrated in the following song:

No. 6. The Wonder-boy and His Father (a)

(Catalogue No. 1215)

Recorded by PETER HAMMON

Voice ♩ = 112
Rattle ♩ = 112
Rattle-rhythm similar to No. 4

Analysis.—This song may be characterized as exclamatory. It contains many short phrases and short rests which were clearly given. The slower tempo of the third period is interesting, also the fact that the period, or section, is entirely on one tone. We note that the words of the song relate the action of the boy in bringing up his father from the ashes and returning him thither. Ascending and descending intervals are equal in number and almost half the intervals are fourths. Next in frequency is the minor third, and the song contains only one progression of a whole tone. Thus the progressions are larger than in a majority of songs of this group.

The boy traveled on, but he was not satisfied. He said that if he could only bring back his father once more and talk with him again he would be entirely satisfied. So he brought back his father a second time, and they wept in each other's arms. After the boy had been with his father a length of time he was satisfied. Then his father said, " During my life I stored a quantity of dried deer meat and other provisions. They are at a certain mountain (named). You are to go there, take everything that I stored, and use it as food on your travels."

The boy replied, "No. What you did and what you wore and what you stored away I do not want to take. I have my own power to go about and provide for myself." So he sent his father back, with dust and clouds and thunders roaring, going down into the earth forever.

The next story is concerning the second restoration of the boy's father. Other songs of this part of the series were not recorded.

No. 7. The Wonder-boy and His Father (b)

(Catalogue No. 1216)

Recorded by PETER HAMMON

Analysis.—The rhythm of the rattle is more irregular in this than in the song next preceding, and the song opens in the same agitated manner, but the second period (B) is calm and restful, suggesting the boy's resignation to the final departure of his father. This period contains only progressions of a whole tone. The rhythm of the rattle was uniform throughout the renditions of the song.

After sending his father away the second time the boy traveled on with no particular objective and finally arrived at the Colorado River. He traveled southward to see if he would come to a narrow place where he could cross the river. Finding none, he turned toward the north. He stopped and looked at the river with wonder. He saw a piece of petrified wood and wrapped up his few belongings and started across the river on the wood. Finding this was not like other wood but was sinking, he tried to hold it up, but just as he was about to drown he was caught by a whirlpool and carried to the other edge of the river. After getting out of the water and putting on his clothes he took one step and was on top of the mountain called Avi'makxĕ'k, which is between Pĭka'tco and the present town of Parker. After standing there quite a length of time he wondered whether his uncle Hatpa'akwa's (Coyote) meant what he said when he told him, "In your travels through deserts and unknown lands if you should happen to swallow your saliva you will become lost in your wanderings." While at this mountain the saying of his uncle came repeatedly to his mind, though he knew where he was and knew the name of the mountain. He said it was his country and that the mountain belonged to him. (The song containing this was not transcribed.)

Then he thought about another place similar to the place where he was. He thought of going there and staying a night, but he changed his mind and thought of another place to the west. He decided to go to this place and started to run down the mountain. Immediately he was at that place, admiring the mountain called Celai't. This narrative is contained in the following song:

No. 8. The Wonder-boy on the Mountain

(Catalogue No. 1217)

Recorded by PETER HAMMON

Analysis.—The uneven rhythm of the drum was maintained in all renditions of this song, indicating that the drum conformed to the melody instead of being an independent rhythm. This is noted in many songs herewith presented and is contrasted to the songs of many tribes previously recorded in which the drum was an independent expression, having its own tempo and rhythm. The peculiar measure lengths of this song were also found in all the renditions. This begins and ends on F, which is the middle tone of its compass. It contains only two intervals larger than a minor third, and about 73 per cent of the intervals are whole tones.

As he stood there he thought that if he started from there and went toward Pĭka'tco, it would be a short cut for him to go through the present site of Yuma and to a certain lake. Then he thought of another place on the east side of the river and decided to go there. He started east toward this place. Finally he came to a place now called Avi'apsĭñ. Then he said, addressing the place, "If I were to call you by a word in my language I would call you Awi'apsĭ, but when the coming generations name you they will call you Avi'apsĭñ." (This song has the same melody as the preceding and was not transcribed.)

After naming this mountain the boy stood there and thought of another place where he wanted to go, because he was not satisfied with any of these places. He traveled on until he came to a place called A'màtiya', meaning Earth-mouth.

No. 9. The Wonder-boy on His Travels

(Catalogue No. 1218)

Recorded by PETER HAMMON

Voice ♩ = 108
Rattle ♩ = 108
Rattle-rhythm similar to No. 4

Analysis.—In this song the Wonder-boy is proceeding on his travels and we find the melody monotonous and the rattle in a steady rhythm of quarter notes. The song contains three periods, the third being shorter than the others and having a more energetic rhythm but no higher tones. The compass of the melody is only five tones and, like the song next preceding, it begins and ends on the middle tone of the compass. Ascending and descending intervals are about equal in number, and with one exception the intervals are minor thirds and major seconds.

He stood there a while and then saw something which seemed to be moving toward the other bank of the slough. It was dressed entirely in bamboo and it had rings on its fingers made of bamboo and it wore bamboo sandals. It also had one bamboo sticking up in its hair like a feather. He said to himself, " I will hide behind this place and catch him. If it is an animal I will keep it for a pet, and if it is a human being I will consider him a friend." While he was hiding there the moving object was coming nearer. It was like the Wonder-boy, only dressed differently. It was his half brother A'xtak-wa'some, who had as much medicine power as he himself possessed. The boy did not realize this, and when the stranger came near his hiding place he started to seize him. To his surprise the stranger suddenly vanished and then appeared on the lowland at the other side of a slough. Then Pokohan recognized him and said, " There is something I wanted to say, and it is this: I am your half brother, and the person who has told me this is my paternal uncle Hatpaakwas."

No. 10. The Wonder-boy Meets His Brother

(Catalogue No. 1219)

Recorded by Peter Hammon

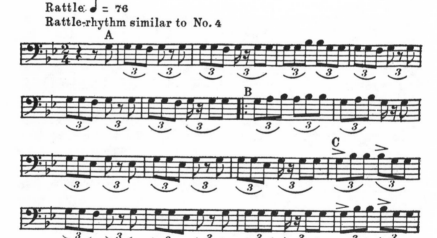

Analysis.—In this song the Wonder-boy meets his half brother and the song contains the exclamatory quality that marked the song of his meeting with his father. Several tones are strongly accented and there are many short phrases separated by rests. The keynote appears to be G, which is in the middle of the compass of the song

and occurs as its first and last tone. Major thirds and major seconds
each occur seven times in both ascending and descending progression. This is the most frequent occurrence of the major third in
the entire group of songs, this interval being omitted from many
songs. In this melody the minor third occurs about half as
frequently as the major third.

The stranger said nothing but stood there with tears running
down his face. There was talk of bringing Hatpaakwas himself
to settle the matter but Pokohan said, " Our uncle is much older than
we are and he was present when you were born; he even took you in
his hands." After the stranger was convinced that he was half
brother to the boy, Pokohan took off his garment, wrapped it on
a stone and threw it over to the stranger on the other side of the
slough. The stranger replied, " I understand how it is, and you
show me much respect, as though I were your half brother, but as
you have seen I have nothing to give you in return, for I wear
nothing but this bamboo." Then he took the garment, put it on
his shoulder and started west while Pokohan went toward the south.
After Pokohan had traveled a distance he stopped and looked toward
where his half brother was going and said, " I will sing for him for
the last time." In this song he calls his half brother by his name,
Ahtakwasome, and says that he is going toward the west. The
melody is a duplicate of the preceding and not transcribed.

Then Pokohan started as though he were going to some particular place. He went until he came to a certain place and there
was a jack rabbit sleeping on the road. He almost stepped on it
and it was frightened and started to run toward the mesa. Then
it stopped and stood on its hind legs and looked at the boy. This
frightened Pokohan, for he was still a little boy and he thought the
jack rabbit was going to catch him. Then he said, " I will destroy
all this grass that you feed on so that you can never come here
again to feed." Yet the boy knew that the grass would grow
again if he destroyed it.

No. 11. The Wonder-boy Meets a Jack Rabbit

(Catalogue No. 1220)

Recorded by PETER HAMMON

Voice ♩ = 112
Rattle ♩ = 112
Rattle-rhythm similar No. 4

Analysis.—Only three tones occur in this song. The drum is in continuous quarter notes, this beat being steadily maintained during a 5-8 followed by a 3-8 measure. Attention is directed to period C, which begins with a 4-measure phrase followed by two measures differently accented; these measures being followed by four measures in the original rhythm.

The boy lighted the grass and it started to burn. Then he said, " If I could only get rid of my hair, so it would not be so heavy in my travels! " So he put his head down in the fire and burned off all his hair. He took the little bamboo (to prevent thirst) and put it in his mouth, and he took the belt (to prevent hunger) and put it around his waist; then he put the war bonnet on his head, but it would not stay on because he had no hair. When he saw this he said, " Why didn't I think of this before? I will have no more use for this war bonnet." But on second thought he spit on the palm of his right hand, put the war bonnet on his right hand and then on his head, and it stayed on. He stood there, shook his head, and said that it was all right.

No. 12. The Wonder-boy and His War Bonnet

(Catalogue No. 1221)

Recorded by PETER HAMMON

Analysis.—This song contains the exclamatory phrases similar to those noted in Nos. 6 and 10. The song has a compass of five tones, the lowest of which is the keynote, but the song begins and ends on the middle tone of the compass. The period B is entirely on one tone, and the melody progresses entirely by major and minor thirds. The drum is in continuous quarter notes except that the beat on the final count of a measure is sometimes omitted.

He started again on his travels and came to a big " wash " and he traveled in that until he came to a narrow place. There he heard a low sound that still was loud. He lay and watched until this sound came up to him and he found it was made by a wild cat. He called the name of the wild cat, Naxmĕ', and said that its body was striped and its eyes shone. This was the first naming of the animal.

No. 13. Song Concerning the Wild Cat

(Catalogue No. 1222)

Recorded by PETER HAMMON

Analysis.—A song concerning a wild cat has not previously been recorded and we look for some peculiarity of rhythm or melody. The drum was clearly audible, and its irregular rhythm is transcribed as it occurred in all the renditions. A 5–8 measure appears four times in the first period, always on the same tone. These features are somewhat unusual. The second period is different in rhythm and less active in its melody progressions. The melody tones are of the minor triad and fourth and the song has a compass of five tones.

Farther on he met a little humming bird and it was making its own sound. It sounded as though there were more than one. When the sound came nearer he saw that it was nothing but a little humming bird, so he stood there and gave it the name of Nakui'x. It is interesting to note the humming, monotonous form of the next song.

No. 14. Song Concerning the Humming Bird

(Catalogue No. 1223)

Recorded by PETER HAMMON

Analysis.—The peculiar sound made by a humming bird is suggested by this melody, the semitone, which is somewhat unusual in Indian songs, comprising about one-third of the progressions. No interval larger than a minor third occurs in the song. The change of tempo in the second period is interesting and was given in all the renditions. The drum beat is somewhat irregular. Cf. No. 76, which is also concerning a humming bird.

He journeyed farther and heard another sound. It came from an insect (horsefly) which he named Huau'. This little insect was in a plant called a mountain star and the boy did not see the insect, but he heard a strange, loud sound coming from the plant. In the song he described the insect and mentioned its wings and its eyes, as well as other characteristics. The song had practically the same melody as that concerning the humming bird and it was not transcribed.

The series could have been greatly extended, the traveler meeting many other insects and visiting other mountains. The portion of the series herewith presented seems, however, to be sufficient for the present purpose.

YUMA CORN DANCE

Several dances associated with the Memorial ceremony were held previous to that event, the most important being the Corn dance (Akil). Corn is mentioned in the Akil songs and the dance was connected with the securing of an abundant crop. Katco'ra (pl. 27, *a*), who recorded the songs of this dance, also assisted the writer by going to the houses of singers living at a considerable distance, persuading them to record songs, and in some instances bringing them to the place where the songs were recorded. He said that he had been a "helper" at the Corn dance and his power was such that his singing of these songs caused the corn to grow faster. The songs began by telling of the planting of the corn, the gradual opening of the leaves, the appearance of the tassels, and the full development of the corn up to its maturity. Several tribes were often in attendance and "each tribe sang of the corn in its own language and in its own way."

In the old days the Yuma, as already stated, were scattered over a wide area, some living in the Gila Valley north of their present abode, some living farther south, and some farther west. They met for the Corn dance, which began when the corn was about 10 inches high and continued until the corn was ripe, which was from four to six weeks.

Those who danced the Akil were "dressed up to look as fierce as possible." Their faces were painted with clay and their hair was arranged high in a pile, willow bark being used in this style of hairdressing. At the beginning of the Akil a meeting was held under a desert shelter decorated with green. (This structure is commonly called a shack.) The people of each village came by themselves, led by a singer, and they all sang as they advanced.

The Akil was danced by both men and women, standing side by side in four or five circles, one inside the other, while the singers were in the middle of the innermost circle. The singers usually comprised two men, with one woman as a helper. Additional women singers are mentioned in connection with No. 17. The songs were accompanied by the shaking of gourd rattles. The dancers did not stand alternating men and women, and they might hold hands or not, as they chose. Much individuality of motion was permitted, as it was said that "some danced up when others were down or bent backward." At first the circles moved in the same direction and a characteristic of the dance was the changing of direction by alternate circles. This was done during songs Nos. 17 and 18. Many other dances were held during the time that the people were together, different singers and dancers taking part.

When the corn was ripe it was cut, placed in a pile, and divided among the people. At the final meeting a speech was made announcing the Kàrok, which began four days afterwards, according to the native reckoning, which includes the first and last days of the four. The person who arranged for the Akil expected to take part in the Kàrok and at its final dance he collected paints, beads, and other articles to be used in the ceremony, the persons who attended the dance contributing these materials.

The Akil in its full form is said to have been given " not so very long ago " with Maricopa, Mohave, and other tribes in attendance, but at the present time the singing and dancing lasts only a week, and has no significance.

The songs of the Akil are in pairs, the first song having words and the second having no words. Katcora recorded one pair of songs, and thereafter sang only the first song of each pair. The words of these songs are in what is known as the " old language." The singers repeat the songs by rote and have a general knowledge of their meaning, but the language is obsolete. It appears that, as in many of these songs, the words are descriptive of action which either is taking place or is supposed to have taken place among mythical personages. The first song was said to state that a certain group of people had arrived and were singing and dancing.

No. 15. Corn Dance Song (a)

(Catalogue No. 1231)

Recorded by KATCORA

Rattle-rhythm

Analysis.—This song consists entirely of 2-measure phrases. The periods A and B each contain four of these phrases and period C contains six, the last two having no rest in the final measure. The song is characterized by the descending third at the close of these phrases, which was always sung glissando. As in many of these songs, the most pleasing portion of the melody is in period C. In two respects this melody is unusual. The lowest tone of the compass is the first and last tone in the song, and 86 per cent of the progressions are fourths and major thirds.

This was followed by a song which had no words, but has the same melody, being the second of the "pair." Katcora next recorded a song which says that after the people arrived they circled around the shack, singing and dancing.

During the two songs next following the alternate circles reversed the direction of their motion. These were the only songs during which this change of direction occurred.

No. 16. Corn Dance Song (b)

(Catalogue No. 1232)

Recorded by KATCORA

Voice ♩ = 88
Rattle ♩ = 88
See rattle-rhythm below
Irregular in tonality

Rattle-rhythm

Analysis.—This melody is classified as irregular in tonality. In order to indicate the tones which were sung by the Indian the song is transcribed with a signature of five sharps. It will be noted that the tone B does not occur, the melody tones being D sharp, E, F sharp, and G sharp. There is a plaintive effect in the frequency of semitones which is somewhat unusual in these songs, comprising 19 of the 26 intervals. The rests were given uniformly in all the renditions. The rhythm of the rattle was different from that in the preceding song and was maintained with clearness.

The interpreter said, "When he shakes the rattle down it is the signal for the women singers to begin. The people dance moderately while the men are singing, but at the change to the women singers the leader says, 'Dance harder. Do your very best.' So they all dance harder."

No. 17. Corn Dance Song (c)

(Catalogue No. 1233)

Recorded by KATCORA

Voice ♩ ＝ 92
Rattle ♩ ＝ 92
See rattle-rhythm below

Rattle-rhythm

Analysis.—This song contains the tones C sharp, D sharp, E, F sharp, and G sharp, and progresses chiefly by minor thirds. The sound of the rattle was synchronous with the voice and occurred only on the first of the measure. As in all songs of this group, the rests were given with much distinctness. Period B consists of four phrases, the second of which is similar to phrases in A, while others differ slightly in rhythm. Each period of the song was repeated several times.

The next song mentions the clouds of dust that arise as the people dance.

No. 18. Corn Dance Song (d)

(Catalogue No. 1234)

Recorded by KATCOBA

Voice ♩ = 96
Rattle ♩ = 96
Rattle-rhythm similar to No. 15

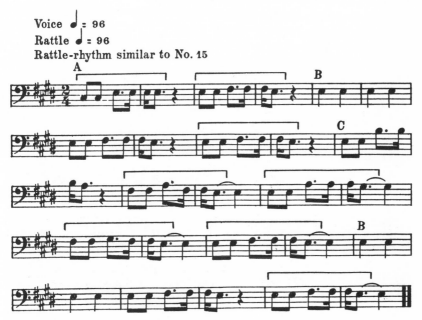

Analysis.—The manner of singing this song was marked by precision and a decided accent. The keynote is regarded as E, and the song contains all the tones of the octave except the third and seventh. The period marked A was sung six times, followed by B sung once, after which A was sung four times, followed by B and C. The only differences in the repetitions was that in the sixth repetition of A the last two measures were omitted, which may have been due to the length of the words. While the rattle could not be distinguished in every measure, it appears to be in the rhythm indicated. About three-fourths of the progressions are whole tones.

The words of the final song state that the people are dancing around in a circle.

No. 19. Corn Dance Song (e)

(Catalogue No. 1235)

Recorded by KATCORA

Voice ♩ = 100
Rattle ♩ = 100
Rattle-rhythm similar to No. 15

Analysis.—This song contains short phrases followed by rests, suggesting No. 15. It has a compass of five tones and contains all the tones in this compass. In a majority of this series of songs the ascending and descending intervals are similar if not equal in number, but in this instance one-half of the upward progressions are major thirds, which do not occur in downward progression, and two-thirds of the downward progressions are whole tones, which occur only twice in upward progression. This gives a rather unusual interest to the melody.

YUMA HUMAN BEING DANCE (PI'PA)

A dance frequently held before the Kàrok instead of the Akil is the Pi'pa, or Human Being dance. This may also be used at a social gathering, and on such an occasion the young men and women take part; but if it is given before the Kàrok it is danced only by older people who are relatives of the persons to be honored, or commemorated, in the Károk. Like the Akil, it ends four days before the beginning of the Károk. The instrument used to accompany the songs is the " spice-box rattle," consisting of a small tin box containing BB shot and pierced with a stick which serves as a handle. This rattle is used with no other songs. The singers are usually 6 to 10 in number and sit on a long bench. (Fig. 4, *c*.) The leading singer has the loudest rattle—not the largest but the one containing the most shot. He sits in the middle of the row and his two best assistants are seated one on each side. The other singers are known as " helpers." The dancers move in two elliptical paths in front of the singers. The men dance nearest to the singers and move face forward. The women move sidewise, facing the singers continuously. (Fig. 4, *a*, *b*.) The number of women dancers is usually larger than the

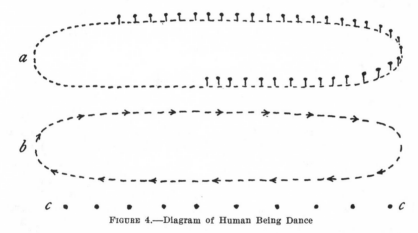

FIGURE 4.—Diagram of Human Being Dance

number of men. The dance is so lively that the dancers are said to have both feet off the ground at the same time, leaping into the air.

When this dance precedes a Károk it is the present custom to begin the dance about noon and continue for two or three hours. When the leading singer sees that all the people expected at the gathering have arrived he begins a certain song. This is the signal for the dance to cease. The women then begin to wail and the whole company begins to cry. This is continued during the entire day, and at its close the speaker announces that the Károk will begin in four days.

YUMA MEMORIAL CEREMONY (KÁROK)

The annual observance of this ceremony is continued by the Yuma at the present time (1922). In some respects the ceremony resembles the Chippewa " restoration of the mourners " and the Sioux ceremony of "releasing the spirit." [25] It terminates the period of mourning, and the preparations occupy the attention of the family and friends of the deceased during the early months of their bereavement. The phase of the ceremony peculiar to the Yuma is the public burning of "images" of the deceased persons, after which the dead are never mentioned. There is considerable expense connected with the making of the images and the gifts to the dead, which debars some of the poorer members of the tribe.

The decision that the deceased shall be represented in the Kårok is made at the time of a cremation. Relatives of the deceased then reserve part of his clothing to be placed on the image that is to be burned. Some time before the Kårok a meeting is held and each person brings a gift of clothing to be put on the image. They all wail and cry as at a cremation. One man is appointed to keep all this clothing, which he takes home and locks in a trunk. The man assuming this responsibility must go without salt or lard for four days and bathe every morning, in order that the spirits of the dead may not trouble him.

Certain materials used in the Kårok, such as native paint or eagle feathers, must be obtained from the vicinity of Needles or Parker, and a messenger is sent to obtain them. This costs two or three horses and a quantity of beadwork or other goods. The messenger announces the Kårok to persons living in that vicinity and tells the time of the ceremony, so they can attend if they wish to do so.

The images used in the Kårok are made to look as much as possible like the persons they represent, both men and women. The work is done by men who are experts and are not paid for their services. One mourner usually provides several images. Thus if a man intends to take part in the Kårok by providing the image of a parent, he is required to provide also the image of another adult relative who has died recently, and if he can afford it he is expected to provide many other images.

In his preparation for making the image a man skilled in the art will go to the relatives and ask how the deceased was accustomed to paint his or her face, and to make any other inquiries that will assist him in securing a likeness. The images are almost life-size. At the present time the framework for the body is made of a board, but in the old days the entire figure was made of cottonwood. The foundation for the head is made of a section of willow log which is made smaller for the neck and attached to a thick board, of such a length as to make the image approximately the height of the person when in life. Projecting crosspieces for the shoulders and hips are

---

[25] Cf. Bull. 53, pp. 153–162 and Bull. 61, pp. 81 to 84.

attached to the board   (Fig. 5.)   This much of the work of pre-
paring the image is done before the time of the ceremony.

The Human Being dance, ending four days before the Károk,
is so timed that the Károk will begin on the day when the moon
rises as the sun sets.   As the Károk lasts four days, this will give
the light of the full moon for the dance and ceremony of the final
day.   Thus if the Human Being dance ends on Monday, the Károk
begins on Thursday, terminating on Sunday night, the ceremony
including the dawn of Monday.   With this sequence of days the relatives of the persons to be honored would gather on Wednesday and
the shack for the lamentations would be built on Thursday.   This
shack was made of green willows and under it the
crying would continue for four days and nights.

The entire company would have gathered by Friday night or early Saturday morning.   The event
of Saturday was the building of the shack where
the ceremony would be held.   This was made of
very dry arrow weed and dry poles.   There was
a prescribed manner for gathering this material.
The persons going to secure it went together for a
certain distance, then separated into two groups,
one going one way and the other going another, but
both traveling toward the east.   About noon they
met at the place where they had separated and returned together, bringing the material.   Then they
went back to the green willow shack.   Certain men
built the ceremonial shack in the afternoon.   This
was oblong in shape, the length extending north
and south.   (Fig. 6.)   They rested that night and
went into the ceremonial shack early Sunday morning.

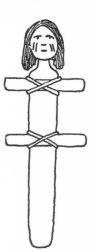

FIGURE 5.—Frame
for i m a g e in
memorial cere-
mony

During Saturday night the preparation of the images was completed,   This was done in a very secluded place, perhaps a mile
from the place where the ceremony was to be held.   The making
of the framework has been already described.   The final work consisted in the modeling and painting of the face, the placing of the
hair, and the clothing of the image.   The round wooden ball which
formed the framework of the head was covered with a reddish gum
made by boiling the root of arrow weed and mashing it.   This was
modeled while warm and made to represent as nearly as possible
the features of the deceased person.   It is said that a striking resemblance was often attained.   A hole was made in the top of the
head, the hair was inserted and brought down around the face,
which was painted in accordance with the custom of the person
when in life.

On Sunday morning the relatives of the persons to be honored and all the company are gathered in the green willow shack, and the images are brought thither from the east, usually a distance of about 100 yards. Each image is brought by a " carrier," who holds the image in front of him, grasping it with both hands by the cross-bar at its hips. They " dance " the images up and down as they advance. In front of the images are the singers walking in a line, and the speaker is usually at the right of this line of singers. The strange procession pauses at four places on its way to the shack, and the speaker makes a speech in the " secret language." This is a formal speech, repeated by rote, and mentions the " wind directions." After each speech the singing is resumed, the images are " danced," and the procession moves forward.[26] During this time the relatives are facing the east, crying and lamenting.

The images are brought into the shack, the carriers " stand them in a row " in the middle of the shack, cover them with a sheet, and go away. The relatives then stand, each near the image of his or her dear one, and cry the rest of the day. For a little time they have looked upon familiar features and garments, now concealed by the white cloth. In a few hours they will see all this consigned to the flames, and forever after they will be forbidden to mention or to weep for the dead. All the memories of the cremation crowd upon them. It is a drama of primitive intensity. During this day there takes place an enactment of scenes associated with the warpath. Certain persons have been asked to take charge of this and are selected from among the older members of the tribe. They are divided into two parties, one representing the Yuma and the other the enemy. They enact the scouting and trailing of the enemy and a " sham battle."

On Sunday evening, just after sunset, a ceremony is begun preliminary to the burning of the images, which takes place early the next morning. The singers take their places in the shack, standing in three lines which extend north and south. The leader is at the center of the middle line with one helper at each side. (Fig. 6.) There are about 10 men in this line and they face the east. Another line of about the same length stands fronting them and thus faces the west. Back of the line in which the leader stands are an indefinite number of singers also in a line facing east. These comprise the younger singers. When the singers sit down they sit on their heels, rising at a signal from the leader who holds the rattle. Joe Homer is in charge of the ceremony at the present time. Although he is blind he has such a clear mental perception of the tempo of the songs and the proper length of time between each song that, at a

---

[26] Luke Homer, the writer's interpreter, has acted as a carrier of the images.

recent ceremony, he led the songs beginning at sunset and concluded them within five minutes of 12 o'clock. He received these songs from his father, Charles Wilson (pl. 1), who recorded many for the present work (Nos. 20–26, 40–56). Wilson said that the Creator commanded the Yuma to have this ceremony and gave them the songs, which they still use. The meaning of the words has been forgotten, but the order of the songs is preserved and the words are repeated by rote. As stated elsewhere, no group of these songs contains more than four and some contain only two or three songs. Each must be sung four times, after which the leader may end the singing at any desired time. These are the only songs ended in this manner. A further peculiarity of these songs is the prolonging of the final tone in a nasal humming sound. These songs, like those of the Akil, are in pairs. The three songs next following were sung at about midnight and the next two songs constitute a pair.

No. 20. Memorial Ceremony Song (a)

(Catalogue No. 1189)

Recorded by CHARLES WILSON

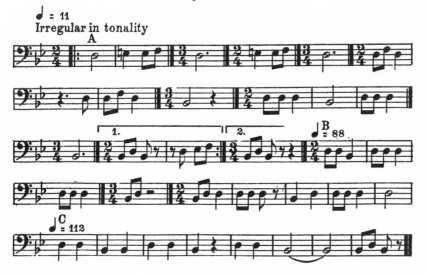

Analysis.—This is the first of a series of seven songs which appear to be based upon successive intervals rather than upon a relation of the tones to a keynote. This song is classified as irregular in tonality. The signature of two flats indicates the pitch of certain tones, but does not imply an established key. A descending fourth is used effectively in many of these songs. The tones of the present melody are D, E, F, suggesting the key of D minor; a few measures later, however, the melody descends to B flat and the remainder of the melody consists of the tones B flat and D. The change of tempo is unusual and interesting, with the return to the original tempo at C. The final section of the song is characterized by quarter notes. Ascending and descending intervals are equal in number and consist chiefly of major thirds, this interval constituting 67 per cent of the entire number of intervals.

No. 21. Memorial Ceremony Song (b)

(Catalogue No. 1190)

Recorded by CHARLES WILSON

Analysis.—The principal intervals in this song are the minor thirds F sharp–A and C sharp–E. The tone B in the seventh and fourteenth measures seems to have little relation to the rest of the song. There is something strangely impressive in the short, monotonous phrases of the latter part of the song and the ascent to the final tone, which is prolonged to a length of four measures.

No. 22. Memorial Ceremony Song (c)

(Catalogue No. 1191)

Recorded by CHARLES WILSON

Analysis.—The keynote of this song occurs only in the fourth measure, this occurrence being on the last count of the measure. This initial interval of a major third, however, provides an opening which is in contrast to the song next preceding. About two-thirds of the remaining progressions are minor thirds between the upper tones of the major triad. The tone B, occurring about midway through the song, gives the slight variation in interest that often appears at this part of an Indian song.

A small bell is rung at exactly midnight. At some time between midnight and the procession of the images there is a dance in which each man is given a downy white feather. They receive these while seated flat on the ground and dance in that position, holding the feather inclosed in their hands. The dance consists in thrusting the head forward and drawing it back, leaning forward and then leaning back. The leader of the singers is the only man with a rattle, and he directs the motions of the entire company, while his helpers, usually two to four in number, sing with him. The next three are songs of this dance and form a group, the motions of the people being the same with all these songs. Different motions were used with other groups of songs.

No. 23. Memorial Ceremony Song (d)

(Catalogue No. 1192)

Recorded by CHARLES WILSON

Analysis.—The tones of this melody consist almost entirely of the two upper tones of a major triad, and therefore a large proportion (about 70 per cent) of the intervals are minor thirds. The keynote occurs only as a short unaccented tone and the sixth occurs only once, giving character to the opening of period B. The melody contains many short, monotonous phrases, with little variety in the length of the tones.

No. 24. Memorial Ceremony Song (e)

(Catalogue No. 1193)

Recorded by CHARLES WILSON

Analysis.—There is an effect of sorrow in the progressions of the first seven measures of this song which is continued throughout the melody. This effect seems to lie in the sequence of F sharp–C sharp, followed by E–C sharp. The prolonged tones indicate the period of " dancing the images." Sixty-eight per cent of the intervals are whole tones and 23 per cent are minor thirds. In contrast to several of the Memorial dance songs the keynote of this melody is frequently repeated and strongly emphasized.

No. 25. Memorial Ceremony Song (f)

(Catalogue No. 1194)

Recorded by CHARLES WILSON

Analysis.—This song contains only the tones of the major triad. Its chief interest lies in the predominance of major thirds which constitute five-sixths of the intervals. The measure divisions of the first section (A) are reversed in the second section (B). This is a form of thematic development that occurs less frequently in the Yuman than in other Indian songs under analysis.

Before the images are burned they are carried in a ceremonial procession around the shack. The carriers for the images are usually the same who brought them into the shack, though one or two may be changed. At the proper time they take their places, each standing beside the image he is to carry. When the leader begins the following song each carrier takes up an image, holding it as before by the crossbar at the hips. They begin the circling of the lodge with this song. The action of moving the images in this manner was said to mean " the dead are dancing." On the prolonged tones of the song they " dance " the image three times from one side to the other, stamping the foot on the side where the image rests on the ground. The carriers pause a few seconds and then " dance " the image three times again. Thus they may move the image to the right, then to the left and right, stamping the corresponding feet. The next motion would be to the left, right and left. The image is heavy and its height makes it still more difficult to handle.

No. 26. Memorial Ceremony Song (g)

(Catalogue No. 1195)

Recorded by CHARLES WILSON

Analysis.—The keynote of this song is strongly emphasized, in contrast to several preceding songs of the present series. The second period (B) consists entirely of repetitions of the keynote except for the descending semitones at the close. The measure division of period A is reversed in the middle portion of the song but reappears in the final phrase. The interval of a fourth, frequently noted in songs concerning motion, constitutes 43 per cent of the intervals in this song, the interval next in frequency being a minor third.

In making the circle of the shack they pause and sing a song at each of the four corners. The procession is led by Joe Homer, the blind man, and it is said that he always stops at the right place as he counts the steps from one corner to another. Only one of these songs was recorded. This was the song which was sung when the procession paused at the northwest corner of the shack, and the melody was found to be the same as that of No. 26.

The procession moves around the outside of the shack, the carriers with the images dancing backward and the singers moving forward. After encircling the shack the singers return to their first position and the carriers pause a short distance in front of the shack. (Fig. 6.) After this pause they also enter.

At the east, at a distance from the shack, a group of men are making arrows. Four songs are sung as they put the feathers on four arrows and fasten the feathers by wrapping with green sinew. The arrows are placed upright in the ground in groups of four. Meantime certain men are making a large shield.[27] In old days this

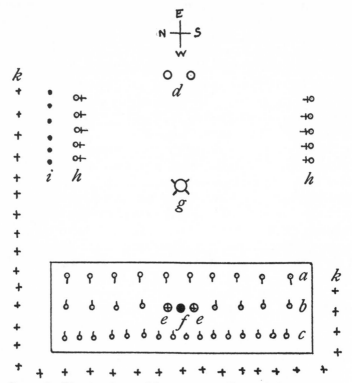

FIGURE 6.—Diagram of memorial ceremony: *a*, Singers facing west; *b*, *c*, singers facing east; *d*, archers; *e*, *e*, assistants to leading singer; *f*, leading singer; *g*, shield; *h*, images; *i*, relatives of persons represented by images; *k*, spectators.

was made of deerskin, but at present it is made of canvas stretched over a hoop, about 3 feet in diameter. The hoop is made of a " very sacred weed " which is pliable. The shield is placed on a light frame, or easel, in front of the shack and at a distance of about 100 feet from it. Four feathers are stuck in the hoop, one song being sung after each feather is put in place.

The singing and dancing continues until about 3 a. m. Four songs are sung and the people form an aisle outside the shack and extend-

---

[27] " This, except for an allusion to its use by the Diegueño, is the most westerly known occurrence of the shield, whose distribution stretches through the Pima and Apache to the Pueblo and Plains tribes. Neither the Yuma nor the Mohave, however, appear to have used the implement very extensively in actual warfare, and there is no mention of any heraldry in connection with it." (Kroeber, Handbook of Indians of California, Bull. 78, Bur. Amer. Ethn., pp. 792–793.)

ing toward the east. The images are in the front row on either side, back of them are the relatives carrying the gifts to be burned with the images, and the people are in the rear. The shack is then set on fire. Four songs are sung, which conclude the singing. Immediately afterwards the archers shoot the four arrows into the shield, rush forward, snatch the shield from its place and throw it into the blazing shack. Then they run down the aisle of people toward a body of water and jump into it. These men wear no clothing except the breechcloth and their faces are painted black and white, each in a solid color except that the men painted white have a black spot on each eyelid. It is required that they go down four times before coming out of the water. The desert nights are cold and this feat is undertaken only by men who have such "medicine power" that neither heat nor cold can harm them.

When this has been done a certain man directs the carriers to take the images straight south to where a pile or "nest" of dry arrow weed has been prepared. The images are laid on the arrow weed face downward, as the body is laid for cremation, and the arrow weed is lighted by the same man who lights the fire at a cremation. The relatives circle around the fire, wailing and throwing gifts into the flames, it being the belief that these gifts go to the dead.

All the people go home directly after the Kàrok. The relatives of persons who have been honored (by the burning of their images), and also the leaders of the ceremony, eat very little food for four days and abstain from lard and salt. In describing the Kàrok it was said, "This was an example to the world that it would be in images that the dead would come back. It will not be the whole person that comes back. The first coming back will be at the time of the cremation, the second will be in images at the Kàrok, but it can be only twice that the dead come back. When they go away after the Kàrok it is forever."

COCOPA CREMATION LEGEND

The translation of this legend and the words of the songs was made possible by the cooperation of two interpreters, Nelson Rainbow translating the Cocopa into Yuma and Luke Homer translating the Yuma into English. This series of songs is called Sà'wi (Cocopa), meaning buzzard, the Yuma term being Sa'wi. Only one Cocopa knows these songs, and he, after some persuasion, consented to sing them. This singer (pl. 27, b) is known by the English name Clam and is called Axlu'm by the Cocopa, this being a mispronunciation of the word "clam." He said that he received this name when he lived by the sea in Mexico. The Cocopa songs were recorded near Somerton, in the extreme southwestern portion of Arizona, where a few Cocopa from Mexico were living but were not yet enrolled as United States Indians. These songs were accompanied by the shaking of a gourd rattle and the words were in an obsolete language. The meaning was known to the singer and the words are given in approximately the words of the interpreter.

In explanation of the songs it was said that in the beginning there were two beings who rose from the bottom of the earth. One caused light and created human beings and the other was destructive. The present series of songs relates to the death [27] and cremation of the second, who will be referred to as Superman. The Cocopa term is Me'sipa, which is used in no other connection. The Yuma term is Koma'stamho. After his death some of the people changed into birds and animals, but the next generation was composed entirely of human beings.

Each song in this group is preceded by the singer's description. This can scarcely be considered as a translation but indicates the content of the words.

The next song states that although the Superman was in a serious condition he would not admit that he was sick. His children, who surrounded him, said they would try again and ask him of his condition.

---

[27] " This concept of the dying god and of the mourning for him is universal among Yumans and Shoshoneans and is probably the dominant and most poignantly felt motive of every mythology in southern California. Its analogue in the Aztec Quetzalcoatl story has already been commented upon, but it is important that no parallel is known among the Pueblos or any true southwestern people. There may have been connections with the central and south Mexican story through Sonora. But except for dim suggestions, the development of the idea is probably local. All the Californians make much of the origin of death. . . . Certain considerations indicate that the dying god concept developed in southern California proper, where its ritualistic counterpart also has its seat, and inclines the balance toward a Shoshonean rather than a Yuman origin for the idea and its principal associations." (Kroeber, Handbook of Indians of California, Bull. 78, Bur. Amer. Ethn., p. 790.)

No. 27. The Illness of the Superman

(Catalogue No. 1256)

Recorded by CLAM

Voice ♩ = 80
Rattle ♩ = 80
See rattle-rhythm below

Rattle rhythm

Analysis.—The rhythm of this song was given with crispness, the rattle coinciding with the voice and continuing through the portions of the measures during which the voice was silent. Progression is chiefly by whole tones which comprise 70 per cent of the entire number of intervals. The remaining intervals consist of 10 major thirds and 6 semitones. Ascending and descending intervals are about equal in number. The song was sung with the repeated portion as indicated, after which the last 12 measures were sung twice. These repetitions were without a break in the tune.

They have failed. In reply to their inquiries the Superman said that he was not sick. In doing so he set an example for wise men to follow, and to this day such men will never admit that they are sick, though they may be in a dying condition. But the children of the Superman still insisted that he was very sick.

No. 28. The Superman Sets an Example

(Catalogue No. 1257)

Recorded by CLAM

Voice ♩ = 92
Rattle ♩ = 92
Rattle-rhythm similar to No. 27

Analysis.—This song progresses chiefly by fourths and semitones, the former being 15 and the latter 14 in number. They occur with equal frequency in ascending and descending progression. Other intervals are minor thirds and major seconds which also are about equal in ascending and descending order, yet the melody is far from being monotonous. Attention is directed to the peculiar phrasing in the seventh to the tenth measures. The first portion of the song (10 measures) was sung three times before the singer proceeded to the remainder of the song. The rattle occasionally omitted one stroke at the end of a measure, resuming with a sharp accent on the first of the succeeding measure.

When it was evident that the Superman was growing rapidly worse his children said, " You are passing away. Your eyes show that you are growing weaker and yet you do not seem to hear what we are saying. We still ask and beg you to speak to us for the last time."

No. 29. The Superman Grows Weaker

(Catalogue No. 1258)

Recorded by CLAM

Voice ♩ = 88
Rattle ♩ = 88
Rattle - rhythm similar to No. 27

Analysis.—This melody lies chiefly below the keynote, which is an unusual formation in the songs under analysis. The only tone higher than the keynote occurs in the opening measures. The song is characterized by a gliding of the voice on descending intervals followed by a rest, the glissando extending below the transcribed tone and gradually trailing into silence. More than half the intervals are whole tones.

A song not transcribed stated that his children continued to beseech him, saying that he seemed to like the ground on which he lay (had no inclination to rise from the ground), and this was a sign that a person would soon pass away. Another song stated that a bug tried to ease him by digging into the ground and bringing up cool sand which it placed on his breast, but this had no effect.

Finally the Superman spoke and said, "I love you, my children, so much that I do not wish to speak, and at the same time I feel as though I were sleepy and could never have any life in me again."

No. 30. The Superman Speaks

(Catalogue No. 1259)

Recorded by CLAM

Voice ♩ = 88
Rattle ♩ = 88
Rattle-rhythm similar to No. 27

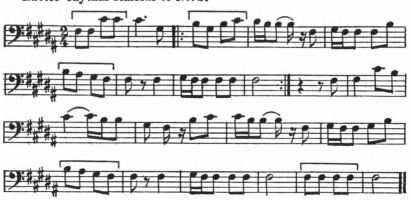

Analysis.—The rhythmic unit of this song is the same as in the next preceding, and the general structure of the two melodies is similar, but the highest tone of the compass occurs more frequently in the present melody. As a further difference between the two songs we note that the present melody contains no change of measure length. Attention is directed to the descending sequence of tones in the sixth measure, which is unusual in recorded Indian songs. The repeated portion was sung three times in each rendition.

The Superman continued, saying, "As I have said before, and in addition to what I have said, I have in my mind the four corners of the earth. Among these I may choose the place to which my spirit will go, but I have not yet chosen."

No. 31. The Four Corners of the Earth

(Catalogue No. 1260)

Recorded by CLAM

Voice ♩ = 84
Rattle ♩ = 84
Rattle-rhythm similar to No. 27·

Fine

Analysis.—The steady rhythm of the rattle was interrupted twice in each rendition of this song, these interruptions being at the voice rest in the seventh measure (one stroke) and in the final measure (two strokes). The repeated portion, including the connective phrase, was sung three times. The song is major in tonality, has a compass of an octave, and contains all the tones of the octave except the fourth. More than half the intervals are minor thirds, and the melody (after the third measure) is based upon two minor thirds— F sharp–A and C sharp–E. The song closes with the ascending interval which characterizes many songs of the present series.

Then the children took hold of his legs and laid him with his feet toward the east. He lay in that position but was not satisfied, so they turned him with his feet toward the north. He said, " No; I do not choose this position." So they turned him toward the west, and after lying there he refused also to follow that direction. So they laid him with his feet toward the south, and in that position he held himself until he passed away, a few moments afterwards. In taking such a position he set an example to coming generations, showing that when they die their spirits will go toward the south.

No. 32. The Superman Dies

(Catalogue No. 1261)

Recorded by CLAM

Analysis.—This song was sung with a quavering tone. (Cf. No. 38.) It contains no interval larger than a major third, the other intervals comprising six minor thirds and eight semitones. In rhythmic structure the song comprises three periods of four measures each.

While the fire of the cremation burned brightly Coyote traveled toward the place. It was said this coyote was " one of the very wild sort that no one ever sees."

No. 33. Coyote Comes to the Cremation of the Superman

(Catalogue No. 1262)

Recorded by CLAM

Voice ♩ = 80
Rattle ♩ = 80
Rattle - rhythm similar to No. 4

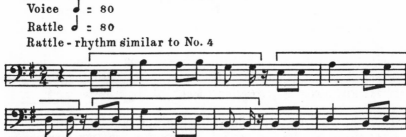

Analysis.—The repetitions of this song began on D instead of E, giving a more harmonic effect. In this, as in a majority of songs in this series, the keynote is near the top of the melody, which ends with an ascending progression. The melody tones are those of the fourth 5-toned scale. The principal intervals are the fourth and minor third, the latter comprising more than half of the intervals, though the song is major in tonality. The song consists of six phrases, all having the same rhythm. Two renditions were recorded, the second ending at the eighth measure of the transcription.

The animals were standing in a circle around the fire and the buzzard asked them all to stand firmly and keep as close together as possible, but there was one animal that was very short. Coyote knew this and planned to break through the line at that point.

After Coyote had arrived he requested the animals in the circle to kindly spread out so that he would have room to get inside and to circle four times around the fire, after which he would find a place where he could stand and cry (after the manner of those attending cremations). But it was whispered from one animal to another to keep their own positions and not move to admit him.

Coyote planned to seize the heart of the Superman and thought that it would not burn him.

No. 34. Coyote Plans to Seize the Heart

(Catalogue No. 1263)

Recorded by CLAM

Voice ♩ = 126
Rattle ♩ = 126
Rattle-rhythm similar to No. 4

Analysis.—Quarter notes and eighth notes, in different groupings, occur throughout this song and comprise the four rhythmic units. Attention is directed to a comparison of these units with their slight difference of note values. The only change from quarter and eighth notes occurs with the use of a half note, midway the length of the song. The rattle is in quarter note values and is continued during the rests, when the voice is silent. As in many songs of this series, the compass of the melody lies chiefly below the keynote.

A song, not transcribed, stated that the female buzzard warned the animals, " Coyote is somewhere near, though we do not see him. We must prepare to prevent whatever he attempts to do."

No. 35. Buzzard Tells the Animals What to Do

(Catalogue No. 1264)

Recorded by CLAM

Voice ♩ = 76
Rattle ♩ = 76
Rattle-rhythm similar to No. 27

Analysis.—This melody is made especially pleasing by the accidental which was clearly given. The phrasing was distinct and the manner of rendition was conscientious. The song begins and ends on the same tone and is based on the fourth 5-toned scale. About half the intervals are minor thirds, though the song is major in tonality. The rattle was in even eighth-note values and occasionally omitted the last stroke in measures similar to the second measure, the voice having a short rest before this count. The sharp, crisp shaking of the rattle added to the effect of this lively melody. The first measure of the first rhythmic unit varied somewhat in this repetition.

No. 36. Coyote Makes a Request

(Catalogue No. 1265)

Recorded by CLAM

Voice ♩ = 76
Rattle ♩ = 76
Rattle-rhythm similar to No. 27

Analysis.—A question and answer seem to be suggested by the two rhythmic units of this melody, equal in length and comprising almost the entire song. The second unit occurs three times on the same tones, which is unusual in these songs and gives an effect of emphasis. Attention is directed to the phrase beginning in the fourth measure which contains a rather impatient sixteenth followed by a dotted eighth note, and therefore resembles the second rhythmic unit. The melody tones are those of the fourth 5-toned scale, but almost half the progressions are minor thirds. These are almost equaled in number by the major seconds, the remaining intervals consisting of eight fourths. The rattle is without interruption and coincides with the voice throughout the song.

The animals kept as close together as possible, but Coyote jumped over the line and seized the heart of the Superman which the fire had not consumed. He jumped out at the same place where he entered the circle and ran as fast as he could toward the east. Then the buzzard said, "I knew something of this sort would happen. Now that Coyote has taken the heart of the Superman, I do not know what to do."

No. 37. Coyote Seizes the Heart

(Catalogue No. 1266)

Recorded by CLAM

Voice ♩ = 88
Rattle ♩ = 88
Rattle-rhythm similar to No. 27

Analysis.—This song is so short that the phonograph cylinder contains 11 renditions. These are uniform in every respect. The only tones are those of the minor triad and the fourth which is sharped in its only occurrence. The melody is well adapted to the words of the song.

When Coyote had traveled a long distance he stopped on a mountain. He ate the heart and became unconscious with a powerful spell cast over him. Immediately he died.

No. 38. Coyote Eats the Heart

(Catalogue No. 1267)

Recorded by CLAM

Rattle-rhythm

Analysis.—The tones occurring in this song are F, G, A, B, and C, with B as a prominent tone. The song next preceding was shown to contain the tones of the minor triad and sharped fourth. This song might be classified as containing the major triad and sharped fourth, but because of the frequency of B natural it is classified as irregular in tonality. The time was not so strictly maintained as in other songs and the tone was quavering as though from weeping. (Cf. No. 32.) Attention is directed to the ascending semitone, which occurs seven times and was sung with a slurring of the voice. The minor third constituted 12 of the 31 progressions. The rhythm of the rattle can be indicated only approximately.

MOHAVE CREMATION LEGEND

This class of songs is called Tumà'nt or (according to Kroeber) Tumanpa. These were sung in the afternoon of a cremation by a close friend of the deceased. A series of seven Tumànt songs was recorded by Billie Poor, a Mohave who lived on the Yuma Reservation. All the phonograph records were studied and two were transcribed, but the melodic trend and general rhythm were so similar that only one is presented (No. 39).

It is said these songs were received in a dream by an old woman who used them in her treatment of the sick. An old man sang the songs for her, but she dictated the order and told him which to sing next.[28] The songs were in regular order and all were accompanied by the shaking of a gourd rattle. When used in treatment of the sick, they could be sung two successive nights. At the present time they are sung in the days that precede the Memorial ceremony and can be sung at any general gathering. The words of the songs are concerning the sickness, death, and cremation of a " deity " called Mà'tàvil', and the legend is a Mohave version of the Cocopa legend immediately preceding.

As an introduction it was said that Màtàvil was sick and it was evident that he could not live long, so the neighbors were called in. The words of the next song are those of the sick man, who realized his condition.

---

[28] This is in accordance with the custom of Owl Woman, a Papago, who treats the sick with songs received in dreams, the songs being sung at her direction by Sivariano Garcia. (See Bull. 90, p. 114.)

No. 39. "I am Going to Die"

(Catalogue No. 1288)

Recorded by POOR

Analysis.—A descending fourth characterizes the first portion of this melody, while the second portion consists chiefly of minor thirds. The performance continued longer than shown in the transcription, the remainder of the phonograph cylinder containing material similar to the transcription with the phrases in irregular order. The most frequent intervals are fifths, fourths, and whole tones.

The succeeding songs relate that he lay down and grew steadily worse. He said, "Tell the neighbors that it is getting dark, so I can not recognize them." In a later song, as he was dying, he said, "You can see what a state I am in. I am struggling and tossing about."

A woman was treating Màtàvil and she felt that her medicine was not working, so she consulted the neighbors. After this consultation she thought that perhaps Badger could help her. So Badger dug under the earth and got some sand and rubbed it all over the sick man. The sand was cool and the sick man thought that he felt better, but afterwards he became worse, and Badger said he could not be of assistance. The man died and the people surrounded him, for they had never seen anything like that before. (It appears this was the first time they had seen death.) It was said, " No one knew what to do. They just stood and looked at him." Then came a very large " screw worm," who said, " I will get a light." He took some willow bark and an arrow-weed stalk, which he twisted. He made a spark and the willow bark took fire, so they could see in the house. The light made by the screw-worm fly was reflected in the sky in the east and looked like a star.

When the sick man was dying he had made a wish. He said, " I wish that Coyote would take after my heart and do what is right." Coyote thought this meant that he was to take the actual heart of the man who died. The people knew that Coyote had the wrong idea, and the old medicine woman tricked him. When the screw worm's light was seen in the east she said to Coyote, " Go, flash your tail in this light and get some fire for the cremation." Coyote went away. While he was gone the people piled the logs, put the body on the pyre, and lighted it with the screw-worm's light. Thus the cremation was started while Coyote was absent. When he returned he found the fire blazing and four tribes assembled to sympathize with the friends of the dead.

The friends stood so close together around the fire that Coyote could not get in. He walked round and round the crowd and as he walked he came to the place where stood Skunk, Coon, Badger, and Gopher. These animals were so short that he leaped over them. The cremation was about half finished. He jumped in, snatched the heart of the body, and ran away with it to the top of a peak west of the present site of Tempe. He rested there and laid down the heart, which stained the peak, so it is known to this day as Vi'ikwahas, meaning Stained Peak, or Greasy Peak. From there he ran to another peak which was on the shore of the ocean. From there he went in to the middle of the ocean, where was a peak on an island, and there he ate the heart of Màtàvil. That island is still called Vi'niwa, from *wa* meaning heart, and *vi* meaning peak.

The Mohave term for Coyote is Huksa'ra, and the Yuma word is Hatĕlwĕ'. Both tribes have many legends concerning Coyote, and " it is known by them that the coyote is the slyest animal living. He is always tricky and into some mischief." This animal is familiar in similar legends among other tribes.

TREATMENT OF THE SICK BY THE YUMA

The Yuma informant selected for this subject was Charles Wilson (pl. 1), who has been mentioned in connection with the war customs, cremation, and Kàrok.

Charles Wilson is a man believed to have supernatural power, and, like men of his character in other tribes, his life is governed by strict discipline. He fasts four times a year, in the spring, at midsummer, in the autumn, and at midwinter, eating neither lard nor salt at these times. On inquiry regarding him it was learned that he does not habitually associate with people. He follows his own life, is industrious, and people seldom see him except when they chance to meet him on the road, but if he chooses to go into a gathering " he always has something funny to say and keeps everyone sociable around him." He is kind to his family and " does not say unkind things about the Government nor about the Indians." His manner is that of a competent, conservative man who commands respect from those around him. In general character he resembles the Chippewa members of the Midewiwin, the Sioux who took part in the Sun dance, and similar men with whom it has been the writer's privilege to confer.

Charles Wilson is said to have such " medicine power " that neither cold nor heat can harm him. Thus he could swim across the Colorado River in winter without danger. It is said that he secures fish when the people are in great need of food. He takes one man from each family and they go down to the river in the early morning. He wades into the water chest deep and catches fish in a triangular scoop net, after which he gives one or two fish to each representative of a family, that all may be fed. It is further said that he " can prevent a gun going off," an incident being related in which a loaded gun failed to go off when he said this would occur.

The Yuma believe that the spirits of the dead are in a spirit land where they live and " have melons the year round." Wilson goes to the spirit land in his dreams. He comes and goes among the spirits, but they pay no attention to him. On his first visit he heard a man making a speech. He could not understand it, though he could see that the spirits knew what was being said.

The father of Charles Wilson had power to treat men who had been shot in the chest. Wilson received power to do the same, receiving this power from his father according to the custom of the tribe. If a father, grandfather, or other near relative wishes to transmit his medicine power to a young boy he causes the boy to have a long illness and cures him, after which the boy is believed to have the medicine power of the older man and receives the songs that accompany its use. Wilson's father had certain songs that he had received in a dream and used in his treatment of the sick, the words of these songs being in a " secret language." These songs were learned by Charles Wilson and are presented as Nos. 40, 41, 42, and 43.

The first use of "medicine power" by an Indian appears to be regarded somewhat as an experiment. (Cf. Bull. 86, p. 81.) Wilson's first treatment of the sick was under the following circumstances: An Indian went to town, entered a store, took a trunk on his back, and started to walk away with it. The storekeeper shot the man through the chest. Wilson's father was summoned and began to treat the man, then he turned to Wilson and said, "Try your power; this is a good case for you to begin on." Accordingly Charles Wilson took the case and cured it, the man living for many years. Wilson also cured a young man who had been shot three times in the chest and once in the arm, and he has power over disease as well as accidents affecting the chest. He was said to have treated double pneumonia and an acute heart attack without singing, but when he treated a man who had chopped off part of his foot he sang the same songs that he uses when treating a gunshot wound in the chest. Numerous other cures were related and it was said that he had never "lost a case." On being questioned he said that he does not believe in what is commonly called "bad medicine" or "bewitching people."

When examining a patient for some uncertain ailment Wilson places his hand on the person's flesh and holds it there until he "gets the sensation in the palm of his hand." Then he moves his hand to another place. Sometimes he says that he can cure the patient, and sometimes he advises the person to go to some one else, known to treat the disease with which he seems to be afflicted. Sometimes he treats headache by sucking blood from the patient's forehead and spitting the blood from his mouth.[29]

Wilson said that he does not "absolutely promise" to cure a sick person when he undertakes a case, but he inspires full confidence in that result, and it is interesting to note in the following description that he requires the sick person to say that he feels better. The treatment is limited to the singing of four songs and lasts about half an hour. Wilson said he requests the spectators to move about in a natural manner during the treatment and especially requests that they appear cheerful. The relatives are forbidden to cry or to smoke, and it is not customary for them to eat or to drink water during the treatment. Wilson said, "I also must go without water and must not drink until the sick person says he feels better. Then I and the patient are at liberty to drink water and have what we want to eat."

---

[29] Kroeber states that among the Yuman tribes "there is no theory of disease objects projected into human bodies. Hence the physician sucks little if at all. The patient's soul, his 'shadow,' is affected or taken away . . . and he counteracts this power with his own, with song or breath or spittle, blowing or laying on of hands or other action." (Handbook of Indians of California, Bull. 78, Bur. Amer. Ethn., p. 775.)

The treatment of a patient unconscious from a gunshot wound in the chest was described as follows: In preparation for the treatment the patient is seated facing the east in the middle of an open space perhaps 8 or 9 feet in diameter. Wilson begins singing when about 25 feet away. He stands facing the north, then the west, south, and east, after which he rushes toward the patient. On reaching the open space he moves slowly in a large circle, gradually diminishing these circles until he stands in front of the patient. Then he goes around to the back of the patient and sings in both his ears, one after the other, then blows in both eyes and both ears, and taps the top of his head. After a rest of perhaps five minutes he sings the second song and repeats the treatment. Before he has given the treatment four times the patient has regained consciousness and vomited clotted blood.

In describing the songs and their use, Wilson said, "When I rush toward the patient my full intention is that he shall regain consciousness. That is my feeling when I sing the first song" (No. 40). This song mentions "an individual who has power." No information was obtained concerning this individual, but it was evidently expected that he would exert his power in behalf of the patient.

Wilson's "feeling" when he sings the second of his four songs (No. 41) is that the hemorrhage will cease. This song mentions a small insect that lives in the water and has power over the fluids of the body. It is believed this insect and the one named in the next song respond when they are called and exert their power to aid the sick man.

His "feeling" when singing the third song is that the patient shall recover the power of motion. This song (No. 42) mentions an insect that "perches anywhere and is very lively. It bobs up and down all the time and has a great deal of motion."

His feeling when he sings the fourth song (No. 43) is that the patient must recover the power of speech. At the end of this song he asks the patient how he feels, and it is said that "he has always answered that he felt better." This song mentions a certain sort of buzzard that has white bars on its wings and flies so high that it is out of sight. This buzzard "sees all that goes on; he watches by day and rules by night." He has great power himself and he also has an influence over the insects named in the previous songs, increasing their power. It is said that "Each of the insects does his best, but it is the buzzard whose great power gives the final impetus and cures the sick man."

Wilson said the patient invariably suffers a recurrence of his difficulty in about six months. If Wilson is notified and gives the patient another treatment the cure will be permanent. No one except himself can give this second treatment and without it the patient will die. An incident was related in which a man belittled the result of the first treatment. Wilson warned him of the recurrence, but the man did not believe it would occur. When it came the man did not send for Wilson and he died in a short time.

No. 40. Song When Treating the Sick (a)

(Catalogue No. 1196)

Recorded by CHARLES WILSON

Analysis.—The opening phrases of this song contain eight measures each. The lengths of the phrases in the remainder of the song are not uniform. The rhythmic unit is that which occurs in all songs used by Wilson when treating the sick. It is an interesting phrase and is both soothing and enlivening. In this song the first measure of the unit is sometimes in 5–8 and sometimes in 2–4 time, probably due to differences in words. The song does not contain the " refrain " or short portion, near the close, which characterizes many Yuma songs, but this may be due to the fact that the phonographic cylinder was not long enough to record an entire performance. The portion transcribed was two minutes in length, after which the phrases succeeded one another in an irregular order. The song as transcribed is major in tonality, contains all the tones of the octave except the seventh, and progresses chiefly by whole tones.

No. 41. Song When Treating the Sick (b)

(Catalogue No. 1197)

Recorded by CHARLES WILSON

Analysis.—The interval of a minor third comprises 71 of the 102 progressions in this song, contrasted with the song next preceding which progressed chiefly by whole tones. This is interesting, as it shows an individuality in songs which appear to be similar and have the same rhythmic unit. The song has a compass of seven tones and is based on the fourth 5-toned scale. The third period (C) contains a change of melodic feeling and no occurrence of the rhythmic unit.

No. 42. Song When Treating the Sick (c)

(Catalogue No. 1198)

Recorded by CHARLES WILSON

Analysis.—The same compass and tone material are found in this song as in the song next preceding. The number of minor thirds is exactly the same, but the progression is reversed, the preceding song containing 34 ascending and 37 descending and this melody containing 37 ascending and 34 descending minor thirds. The preceding song contained 9 ascending and 5 descending fourths and this melody contains 6 ascending and 9 descending fourths. The preceding song contained 45 whole tones, chiefly in descending progression, and this melody contains 36 whole tones, chiefly in ascending order. The portion transcribed is that which arrives at a satisfactory ending, but the performance continued to the end of the phonograph cylinder with the phrases repeated in irregular order and in a monotonous manner. Throughout the Indian songs which have an element of magic we note a monotony with slight unexpected change. Attention is directed to period B, which introduces an emphatic rhythm on repetitions of one tone. This suggests that the medicine man, having begun his work by soothing and cheering the patient, is now becoming somewhat urgent. The rhythmic unit is the same as in other songs of the group and does not occur in the second period.

No. 43. Song When Treating the Sick (d)

(Catalogue No. 1199)

Recorded by CHARLES WILSON

Analysis.—In the final song of this series we find the same rhythmic unit as in preceding songs of the group and the same tone material as in the two songs next preceding. The indeterminate ending also characterizes the song, the portion transcribed being of a satisfactory length, after which the performance seemed to be less coherent, continuing to the end of the phonographic cylinder. The song is characterized by short phrases followed by rests, and we note that after this song the doctor asked the patient if he felt better. The melody is somewhat monotonous and does not contain the repetition of a single tone which marked the preceding song. The general effect of the song is cheerful and the proportion of fourths is less than in the preceding song. The minor third constitutes more than half the progressions, but this interval is not associated with sadness in the Indian songs which have been observed.

YUMA LIGHTNING SONGS

The following group of songs was recorded by Charles Wilson, who also supplied the information concerning them. The name of the group is Hurau′, meaning Lightning. Wilson said that he received the songs in a dream from White Cloud (Akwĕ′kwaxma′l), who controls the lightning, thunder, and storms, and for this reason he regarded them as sacred. He recorded the first two songs on his first visit to the writer's office and the act caused him such anxiety that he could not sleep that night. The purpose of the work was carefully explained and the remainder of the series was recorded without anxiety at a subsequent time.

Wilson said that White Cloud appeared to certain medicine men in a dream and gave them power to bring rain or to cause a sand storm. If a man with this power were with a war party he could summon a sand storm to conceal the warriors. A certain bug has power over the storm. This bug may appear to a man in a dream, go through the following performance, and teach him the songs. In such a dream the bug drags his tail on the ground, wriggles it in some way, and causes the dust to rise. This increases as he speaks and gives commands until the dust raised by his own performance covers the whole earth. Wilson said he had seen a dust storm produced by men with this power, but added modestly, "As to myself, I have been shown only this much, to tell this story of White Cloud at a gathering on this earth."

The narrative embodied in the Lightning songs is concerning the journeys and demonstrations of power by White Cloud as a " wonderchild." Wilson said, " He has only one bow and one arrow. He holds them in his hands, and whenever he swings his bow in any

direction it lightens and when he moves his body it thunders." [30]
The songs are in groups of three, each group having the same tune
but with different words. Only one of a group was generally recorded, though in one instance an entire group of three with the same
melody were found on the phonographic cylinders. The words of the
songs are summarized in the titles and are frequently in the first
person.

No. 44. " I Have Arrived in the Sky "

(Catalogue No. 1200)

Recorded by CHARLES WILSON

Analysis.—The tone material of this song does not conform to any
established key, but the first and third measure in section B suggest
the key which is indicated in the signature. This is used for con-

---

[30] Another informant said that if a medicine man wished to bring on a sand storm he
made a speech known only to himself and then sang a song. Immediately the storm came.
This informant said, " The Lightning story is dangerous." His version was concerning
a boy named Kwayawhumar, who says at the end of the story, that people will always
know where he is but will never see him. This boy " lives up in the sky where it is all
frozen snow; in the spring he goes hunting and every time he draws his bow it causes
lightning and when his arrow strikes something it causes the thunder."

venience in designating the pitch of the melody tones, with D flat as an accidental. The song is unique and worthy of special attention. The first period (A) consists of two phrases, each containing 10 measures. These phrases comprise a repetition of a 3-measure rhythmic unit followed by the second rhythmic unit which contains four measures. The next section (B) opens with four repetitions of the first rhythmic unit, followed by two repetitions of the last part of the second unit, after which the song closes with a recurrence of the 10-measure opening phrase. The remainder of the phonograph cylinder contains a repetition of the song with unimportant changes, such as the substitution of a quarter for two eighth notes. Such changes might be made necessary by the use of different words in repetitions of the song.

No. 45. "The Sky is in Darkness"

(Catalogue No. 1201)

Recorded by CHARLES WILSON

Analysis.—It will be noted that the time unit of this song is half that of the preceding song. As the melody contains the tones B flat, E flat, and A natural it is transcribed with the signature of two flats, but the tone B flat occurs only once in the song. The portion marked B was sung several times, the initial tone being given with clear intonation. Like the preceding melody, this progresses chiefly by whole tones.

The melody of the three next recorded songs is the same. In one of these songs White Cloud says that he has seen a certain mountain (near the present site of Indio) and is traveling toward it. In the next three songs he named the mountain, calling it Avi'tinya'm, which means Dark Mountain. The melody was repeated accurately, and the transcription is from the second of the group.

No. 46. "On Top of His Own Mountain"

(Catalogue No. 1202)

Recorded by CHARLES WILSON

Analysis.—The tone material of this song is unusual and consists of 49 whole tones, 9 fifths, 9 major thirds, and 1 interval of a fourth. The song is transcribed with the signature of three flats as a convenient manner of indicating the pitch of the tones, not as indicating an established key. It is interesting to note the accented tones at the beginning of section C, after which the phrases are similar to those of the first section.

In explanation of the following song it was said that, while the Wonder-boy has traveled through the night Coyote has continually seen the daylight.   Coyote danced and sang this song.

No. 47. Song of Coyote

(Catalogue No. 1203)

Recorded by CHARLES WILSON

Analysis.—This song is supposed to be sung by Coyote and we note an entire change of melodic form and tempo. The phrases are shorter than in the preceding songs and the tempo is slower. The phrase at the opening of section B, designated as the second rhythmic unit, stands out clearly and is followed by repetitions of the first rhythmic unit. The sixth was flatted, except in its first occurrence. More than three-fourths of the intervals are whole tones.

When White Cloud left Dark Mountain he went up into the air, making a path in the sky. At last he found a place in the air which pleased him so well that he called it his home.

No. 48. "At the End of the Path in the Sky"

(Catalogue No. 1204)

Recorded by CHARLES WILSON

Analysis.—In this song we find a dignified, somewhat impressive character befitting a song in which White Cloud announces the place he will call his home. The phrases are short and the song contains no rhythmic unit, yet the rhythm is carried forward with a steadiness that is unusually interesting. As in a majority of other songs of this series, the highest tone occurs in the third section (C). The manner of use of the tone D is interesting. The tone material is that of the key of E minor, but, as in several other songs by this singer, the sequence of the tones is at times rather awkward to our ears. About two-thirds of the intervals are whole tones and 16 are fourths.

The next four recorded songs were not transcribed but are summarized as follows: In the first songs White Cloud says that he has made the path in the sky and found a place which he calls his home, but he wonders how he can make a living. This is a pretense, as he

knows what he will do. The next song is concerning the bats. The
singer said he has noticed the bats in the early night coming out and
dancing as he sings this song. The third song states that as White
Cloud stood in the same place he watched the circling clouds and
thought they were smoke. The words of the fourth song state that
while standing there he saw a bird called Meru'si and asked the bird
concerning its wanderings. The bird answered and said he had just
come from the east.

The remainder of the songs were sung in the latter part of the
night. In the song next following White Cloud expresses himself
as satisfied with all that he has seen and says that he will now
demonstrate his own magic power which will be shown in the sky.

No. 49. White Cloud Declares His Power

(Catalogue No. 1205)

Recorded by CHARLES WILSON

Voice ♪ = 184
Rattle ♩ = 92

Analysis.—In this song White Cloud is saying that he will demonstrate his power, and we note a particularly complicated relation of voice and drum. The latter is in steady quarter notes, but the melody is accented in eighth-note values at the beginning of each phrase, the voice and drum being accented together on the last measure of the phrase. The coincidence on this measure gives an effect of emphasis. Section B is marked by the highest tone in the song, and section C by the longest tone and by a change of rhythm. About half the intervals are whole tones, but the song contains a greater variety of intervals than any other of the series, the intervals comprising fifths, major thirds, minor thirds, and semitones, with one occurrence of a seventh and a fourth.

White Cloud says that he will be known by the lightning, thunder, and rain in the sky, and that these will be continued, though he may go away. During the next three songs he calls the clouds, the lightning, and the high winds. They come at his command and fill the heavens. The third song of the group was not transcribed.

No. 50. White Cloud Demonstrates His Power (a)

(Catalogue No. 1206)

Recorded by CHARLES WILSON

Analysis.—In this and the song next following White Cloud is exerting his tremendous power.   In both these songs the minor third, which has been absent or infrequent in the preceding songs, appears with almost as much prominence as the major second.   The drumbeat in this melody is in interrupted eighths and is especially interesting at the beginning of section D.   The song has a compass of an octave and the difference in pitch between the tones transcribed as F natural and F flat was clearly given.

No. 51. White Cloud Demonstrates His Power (b)

(Catalogue No. 1207)

Recorded by CHARLES WILSON

Voice ♩ = 88
Drum ♩ = 88
Drum-rhythm similar to No. 4

Analysis.—This song is based on the second 5-toned scale and progresses chiefly by whole tones, although more than half the intervals are minor thirds.   No change of time occurs in the song, which is unusual.   The melody suggests little resourcefulness in either rhythm or melodic progression, but the rhythm is interesting and carried forward in a steady manner.

In the song next following White Cloud has returned to his home. He stands there in the sky and sings this song.

No. 52. "White Cloud is Singing in the Sky"

(Catalogue No. 1208)

Recorded by CHARLES WILSON

Voice ♩ = 88
Drum ♩ = 88
Drum-rhythm similar to No. 4

Analysis.—This melody is based on the fourth 5-toned scale and contains three rhythmic units which bear a close resemblance to one another. The first section of the song (A) contains 15 measures, the second (B) contains 13 measures, the third (C) contains 16 measures, and the final section (D) contains 6 measures. These divisions are not arbitrary, but intended to assist the observation of a monotonous melody. This song has a compass of only five tones.

White Cloud has decided to travel again. He intends to go toward the south, and in this song he tells of the proposed journey.

No. 53. "I Will Go Toward the South"

(Catalogue No. 1209)

Recorded by CHARLES WILSON

Analysis.—A form of rhythmic speech is suggested by this melody. The phrases are not uniform in length and were ended crisply. The tones indicated as a rhythmic unit are simply a recurrent phrase, without influence on the rest of the rhythm. More than four-fifths of the progressions are whole tones. Except for the ascent at B, the song contains only the tones E flat, F, and G.

As he passed a certain place in the sky he saw a woodpecker and said, " Now I know that creatures such as you live and roam in a place like this."

No. 54. Song to the Woodpecker

(Catalogue No. 1210)

Recorded by CHARLES WILSON

Voice ♩ = 92
Drum ♩ = 92
Drum-rhythm similar to No. 4

Analysis.—A peculiarity of this song is the occurrence of the rhythmic unit in all its periods and the occurrence of the highest tone in the second period, this being more frequently deferred until the final period. The tones are those of the fourth 5-toned scale which is major in tonality, yet the interval of a major third does not occur in the song.

In the song next following he has gone still farther and come down to the ocean, where he sees the great waves throwing masses of mist into the air. He is now on the earth and he sings this song.

No. 55. Song Concerning the Ocean

(Catalogue No. 1211)

Recorded by CHARLES WILSON

Voice ♩ = 138
Irregular in tonality

No. 55 (Continued)

Analysis.—In this song concerning the ocean we look for some characteristics different from those of the preceding songs, and find a rapid melody consisting chiefly of quarter notes and half notes. The rhythmic unit is very simple. The song has a compass of only five notes and contains three rhythmic units, the second and third rhythmic units having a resemblance to one another. More than half of the intervals are whole tones, next in frequency being the minor third and the fourth. There is a slight swaying in the melody, with little effect of actual motion. Apparently it is the vastness of the ocean that impresses White Cloud, though he mentions the masses of mist.

In the final song he says, " This is the beginning of the clouds, the high winds, and the thunder. I alone can command them to appear."

No. 56. "My Power is in the Sky"

(Catalogue No. 1212)

Recorded by CHARLES WILSON

Voice ♩ = 96
Drum ♩ = 96
Drum-rhythm similar to No. 4

Analysis.—The two rhythmic units in this song differ only in that one has a preparatory tone on an unaccented part of the measure. The song is minor in tonality, with unusual prominence given to the whole tone between the seventh and keynote. With the exception of one ascending fourth the melody progresses entirely by minor thirds and whole tones. These are strangely uniform in number, there being 15 of each interval in ascending progression and 16 of each interval in descending progression.

YUMA DEER DANCE

One of the principal cycles of Yuman songs is that concerning the deer (Akwa'k). This was said to be the only cycle with dancing. A description of the cycle was obtained among the Yuma, with numerous songs, and the dance itself was witnessed among the Yaqui and songs recorded. (See pp. 154–166.) No attempt was made to obtain a comparison of the Yuman and Yaqui legends.

The Yuma cycle of Deer dance songs required one night for its rendition, each part of the night having its own songs. The dance or cycle was said to be based on a belief that the deer has power over certain animals which are mentioned in the songs. These, however, are not all the animals over which the deer has mysterious power. The journey of the deer, described in the songs, is summarized as follows: The deer traveled at night, starting from the tall mountain mentioned on page 139. He traveled in a southwesterly direction and came to the mountains the other side of the present site of Indio. Passing through those mountains, he went to the ocean where " some of the deer became wild elks." From the ocean he turned eastward and when he reached the Colorado River he called it the Red River.

He proceeded eastward until he came to some high mountains which he named Mokwi'ntaor. These can be seen in the east. He went farther east until he reached the high mountains west of Phoenix, and that is the place where the sun begins to shine in the morning. The songs are concerning various incidents of this journey. These contain the characteristics of the Yuman song cycle, including the transformation of the deer and the naming of various mountains.[31] The Deer dance is usually held in summer at the time of a full moon. The men are painted and usually wear an animal's tail or the head of a deer. Sometimes a man wears the whole skin of a wild cat on his head with the paws hanging on each side of his face. The animal's tail is hung at the back of the dancer's belt. The dancers stamp their feet, as in the dances of the Kårok, and when a man stamps his right foot he dips his right hand below his knee and puts his left hand and arm behind him, reversing this when he stamps his left foot. It appears this is not the only motion of the dance, as it is also said that both men and women take part, standing alternately, holding hands and moving sidewise. If there were enough dancers, they formed two circles around the basket drums, one circle moving clockwise and the other in the opposite direction. (Fig. 7, p. 150.) The dancers do not sing. The songs are accompanied by pounding on overturned baskets (p. 24). Three

---

[31] The latter characteristic occurred in the legend of the travels of Elder Brother, recorded among the Papago. (Bull. 93, pp. 25, 26.)

baskets are generally used and four singers are seated at each. The leading singer at each basket strikes the basket with two willow sticks held in his right hand, the others striking it with the palm of the right hand. A leading singer starts the songs and the others join him after a few notes.

The following songs were selected from those which were sung in the several parts of the night. The first songs were said to belong to the early part of the night and are concerning the water bug (mai'lkapi'l), while the mention of the mountain where the deer began his journey occurs somewhat later in the series.

Alfred Golding (pl. 31, a), who recorded these songs, brought his willow sticks and bundles of arrow weeds for pounding the basket, this being his custom when going to places where he expects to sing. They were neatly wrapped in a white cloth.

No. 57. "The Deer Begins His Travels"

(Catalogue No. 1163)

Recorded by ALFRED GOLDING

FREE TRANSLATION

The deer is traveling down from the source of the Colorado River.

Analysis.—The transcription represents the first rendition of this song. The second rendition began with the second rhythmic unit and repeated the closing phrase of the song, thus retaining the 3-phrase form of the song. The next rendition began at the same point, continued for six measures, then repeated these measures and continued to the end, with two additional repetitions of the final phrase. The next rendition was like the second. This is an example of the irregular manner of repeating many Yuma songs. The opening measures are often omitted in the repetitions, and the phrases seem to be repeated according to the fancy of the singer. This melody has a compass of three tones and progresses chiefly by minor thirds. This interval was enlarged by singing the lower note slightly below the indicated pitch. The drumbeat was synchronous with the voice, the strokes being as indicated.

No. 58. "The Water Bug and the Shadows"

(Catalogue No. 1164)

Recorded by ALFRED GOLDING

FREE TRANSLATION

The water bug is drawing the shadows of the evening toward him on the water.

Analysis.—The upward and downward progressions in this melody are equal in number, but the ascending progressions are the more prominent and usually occur before an accented tone. The only tones occurring in the melody are F, A flat, and B flat. The minor third comprises three-fourths of the intervals and is the only progression occurring in and after the fourth measure. As in the song next preceding, this interval was sung slightly larger than the indicated pitch. In some of the renditions the final tone in the second and fourth measures from the end of the song were omitted, the tone A flat being prolonged to the time of both tones in the transcription. This is an example of the slight changes sometimes noted in repetitions of songs. The series concerning the water bug comprises six songs, all of which are minor in tonality.

No. 59. Dance of the Water Bug

(Catalogue No. 1165)

Recorded by ALFRED GOLDING

FREE TRANSLATION

The water bug is dipping the end of his long body in the water and dancing up and down.

Analysis.—The first part of this song comprises three rhythmic periods, each having a rest midway its length. The first period contains four complete measures, the second ends with the eighth, and the third ends with the twelfth measure. The form of the latter part of the song is the same, the three periods being repeated but the melodic progressions being slightly different. The phrases are short and clearly defined. It is interesting to note that this is the dance of an insect, to which such phrases are appropriate. Progression is entirely by major and minor thirds and major seconds. The keynote appears to be G sharp, but instead of the fifth above that tone we find E sung repeatedly and with unmistakable intonation. The prominence of the submediant in minor songs occurs in other songs of this group. Attention is directed to the rests in the drumbeat which were similarly given in all renditions of the song.

No. 60. The Water Bug on the Mountain

(Catalogue No. 1166)

Recorded by ALFRED GOLDING

FREE TRANSLATION

Continuing this motion, the water bug came to a mountain called Avi'herutâ't. Standing on top of this mountain, he is gazing and he smells the breeze from the western ocean.

Analysis.—This and the three songs next following are concerning the water bug and contain many interesting points of resemblance. These songs are minor in tonality and lack the fourth and seventh tones of the complete octave. These are the omitted tones in the fourth 5-toned scale, but their omission in songs of minor tonality is unusual. All these songs progress chiefly by major thirds, end with an ascending progression, and have a compass of seven or eight tones. The pitch of the keynote (G sharp) was remarkably accurate through the series. It is the final tone in all the songs and the first and last tone in this and No. 62. The present song is rhythmic in character, but the rhythmic unit is short and unimportant.

No. 61. The Water Bug Sees a Fish

(Catalogue No. 1167)

Recorded by ALFRED GOLDING

FREE TRANSLATION

While the water bug stands there the ocean seems to draw nearer and nearer, and in the water he sees a fish traveling up and down with the tide. (This fish was said to be shaped like a sunfish but larger.)

Analysis.—The phonograph record of this song shows a remarkable combination of rhythms in voice and drum, the voice being measurable by both eighth and quarter note values while the drum is steadily in quarter-note values. The drumbeat was clear, making transcription possible. No instance similar to this has been recorded by the writer. Attention is directed to the complex idea of the song, in connection with the complexity of rhythms. The melody has a compass of eight tones and, like the other five songs concerning the water bug, is minor in tonality. About half the intervals are minor thirds and the song contains 22 ascending and 21 descending intervals.

No. 62. The Water Bug Stands Upon the Fish

(Catalogue No. 1168)

Recorded by ALFRED GOLDING

FREE TRANSLATION

Standing as in a dream, he came to the ocean and stood on the top of the fish, thinking that he was standing on the ground. Then he found it was moving and said, "This is something alive."

Analysis.—This song is characterized by its succession of quarter notes with the drumbeat coinciding with each note. In this connection it is interesting to observe the words which state that the water bug stood upon the great fish. This song has the same keynote and tone material as three other songs concerning the water bug. The repetitions contain a few unimportant differences, affecting the melody more than the rhythm.

No. 63. The Water Bug Wanders Forever Beside the Sea

(Catalogue No. 1169)

Recorded by ALFRED GOLDING

FREE TRANSLATION

The water bug wanders forever beside the sea. After standing on top of the fish the water bug became black, this being caused by a disease that he took from the fish. Therefore he wanders forever on the shore of the ocean.

Analysis.—The opening phrase of this song occurs only once on the phonograph cylinder. Slight differences of melodic progression occur in the repetitions but the rhythm remains the same. This song contains an unusual number of syncopations which were given with distinctness and in exact time. More than half the progressions are major thirds. A connective phrase was sung between the renditions of the song. Attention is directed to the note preceding the rest, which in every instance was clearly cut, ending in exact time.

No. 64. The Deer is Taking Away the Daylight

(Catalogue No. 1170)

Recorded by ALFRED GOLDING

FREE TRANSLATION

The deer is taking away the daylight. After taking away the daylight he named it darkness.

Analysis.—The interest in this melody is well sustained and the general effect is particularly pleasing. Attention is directed to the break in the rhythm produced by the 5–4 measures. Two rhythmic units occur which have no resemblance to each other. The minor third and major second comprise all except eight of the progressions. The drum was synchronous with the voice, frequent rests occurring as indicated. Although the song has a compass of only seven tones, about two-thirds of the intervals are in descending progression.

No. 65. All is Darkness

(Catalogue No. 1171)

Recorded by ALFRED GOLDING

FREE TRANSLATION

The deer is alone in the darkness, grazing on a lonely plain, near the high mountain (A'vikwa'ame).

Analysis.—The title of this song suggests no action or special interest, and we note that the melody contains no change of measure lengths, moving smoothly along a simple path. The song is major in tonality, containing the tones of the fourth 5-toned scale. Progression is chiefly by minor thirds and major seconds, which are about equal in ascending and descending progression. The second rhythmic unit is an extension of the first, which is an unusual thematic treatment.

No. 66. The Spider Makes a Road

(Catalogue No. 1172)

Recorded by ALFRED GOLDING

After the deer had been in the darkness a long time he asked the spider to have a road made for him in the darkness. The spider made the road and the deer is now traveling on it.

Analysis.—In this song we find a short, crisp unit of rhythm, with interesting interruptions at the ninth, twentieth, and thirtieth measures. The tone material consists of G, with its second, third, and sixth. Semitone progressions comprise about one-fourth of the intervals, the song containing no interval larger than a major third. Attention is directed to the ascending progressions followed by rests, and to the interesting progressions in the third measure from the close of the song.

The road made by the spider was a long thread of spider web. The deer traveled on this until he got out of the darkness. He rolled and shook himself after he reached the daylight. (The song concerning this episode is not transcribed.)

Then he asked various birds and animals to sing or do something characteristic for him, and after each had performed he said, " That is all right, that is all you can do." He requested the blackbird to sing a song for him.

No. 67. Song of the Blackbird

(Catalogue No. 1173)

Recorded by ALFRED GOLDING

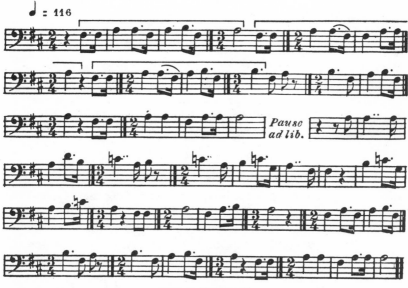

The blackbird is singing and all the blackbirds are dancing on the ground.

Analysis.—This is a fluent melody, containing 73 progressions in 36 measures. The tone material resembles that of No. 44, the song being major in tonality with the seventh lowered in every occurrence. The rhythm of the first measure appears frequently throughout the song. The interval of a fourth is prominent, but the minor third is the most frequent interval, comprising more than half the progressions. The descending fourth followed by an ascending third is interesting and suggests the swiftly sweeping motion of a bird. (Cf. Nos. 72 and 73, which are also concerning blackbirds.)

No. 68. Song of the Buzzards

(Catalogue No. 1174)

Recorded by ALFRED GOLDING

Fine

FREE TRANSLATION

The buzzards are singing and dancing in the sky.

Analysis.—This song is analyzed with D flat as the keynote, but the third and fourth above that tone do not appear. The seventh is flatted in one occurrence. About one-fourth of the intervals are fourths, but in this song concerning the buzzards we do not find the descending fourth followed by an ascending third which characterized the song of the blackbird. The motion of the melody is heavier and there are frequent repetitions of a single tone. This song contains about one-third as many intervals as the song next preceding.

No. 69. Song Concerning the Raven

Recorded by Alfred Golding

(Catalogue No. 1175)

While the buzzards were singing and dancing in the sky the raven tried to dance, too, but he failed and dropped to the ground.

Analysis.—The rhythmic unit of this song resembles the unit of the song of the buzzards but is shorter. The song opens with an ascent of a seventh in two consecutive intervals, which is an unusual beginning. After this opening the melody tones are chiefly a repetition of E, F sharp, G sharp in various sequences. Almost two-thirds of the intervals are whole tones. The song is minor in tonality and is based on the second 5-toned scale.

No. 70. Song Concerning the Deer

(Catalogue No. 1176)

Recorded by ALFRED GOLDING

Voice ♩ = 116
Drum ♩ = 116
Drum-rhythm similar to No. 12

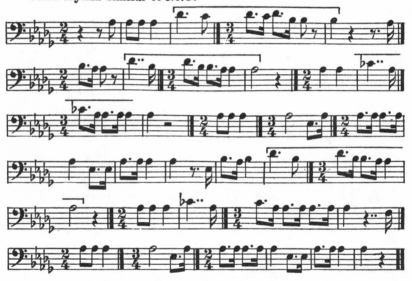

FREE TRANSLATION

The deer turned and asked other animals to sing for him.

Analysis.—This is a particularly free melody, and, as in several others recorded by this singer, the pitch of the lowest tone is such as to make the melody difficult to classify. Thus if the lowest tone in the closing measures were F instead of E flat the melodic structure would be much simpler. The singer seems to have attached slight importance to these tones, or perhaps they were below the natural compass of his voice, as the intonation is not so clear as on the other tones. The seventh is flatted in all its occurrences. The fourth is a prominent interval, but the melody progresses chiefly by minor thirds. The drum is in quarter notes with rests corresponding to rests in the voice.

No. 71. The Howling Coyote

(Catalogue No. 1177)

Recorded by Alfred Golding

Voice ♩ = 126
Drum ♩ = 126
Drum-rhythm similar to No. 12

FREE TRANSLATION

The howling coyote took up common dirt and scattered it toward the sky. He caused the dirt to become stars and the rainbow.

Analysis.—This song concerning the coyote has a compass of only five tones and contains only the tones of the major triad. Sixteen progressions occur, 12 of which are major thirds. Rests are of frequent occurrence, but the rhythmic phrases are not clearly defined. We note that coyote did not sing, but ridiculed the performance of the other animals.

No. 72. The Blackbirds are Dancing

(Catalogue No. 1178)

Recorded by ALFRED GOLDING

FREE TRANSLATION

The little blackbirds are singing this song as they dance around the four corners of the sky.

Analysis.—In this dance of the blackbirds we have a type of melody wholly different from that of the songs next preceding. The melody progresses more widely and freely, and the rhythm is more complicated. The tones contained in the melody are those of the key of D major with G omitted except that C is sung C natural in every occurrence. As C natural occurs so frequently, the song is classified as irregular in tonality. About half the intervals are minor thirds. (Cf. No. 67.)

No. 73. The Dance of the Blackbirds is Completed

(Catalogue No. 1179)

Recorded by ALFRED GOLDING

Voice ♩ = 116
Drum ♩ = 116
Drum-rhythm similar to No. 12
Irregular in tonality

Analysis.—This melody contains the same tone material as the song next preceding and is also classified as irregular in tonality. The melodic structure is based on the three descending minor thirds D–B, C–A, and A–F sharp, ending with a repetition of A. The melody then ascends to E and returns to the former sequence of minor thirds. This "interval structure" usually characterizes songs in which the tones are not referable to a keynote. The rhythm of this song is simple and the rhythmic unit comprises only one measure.

No. 74. The Redbird Speaks (a)

(Catalogue No. 1180)

Recorded by ALFRED GOLDING

Voice ♩ = 69
Drum ♩ = 69
Drum-rhythm similar to No. 27

The red bird was requested to sing, but instead he spoke of his own way of living and said that he lived in the open, among the clouds and the winds. He said that he dreamed of a certain sort of dance and that it was his dance.

Analysis.—In this song we have the expression of a bird that has not been previously mentioned and a melodic structure that is unusual. The song has a compass of seven tones, is based on the second 5-toned scale, and lies entirely above the keynote. From the highest to the lowest tone the melody descends in the first three measures by means of two fourths (one with a passing tone) and a minor third. After a repetition of this interval, the melody ascends to the highest tone and descends in the same manner. A prominence of the fourth has frequently been noted in songs concerning birds. The count divisions in the song are short and the rhythmic unit comprises half the melody.

No. 75. The Redbird Speaks (b)

(Catalogue No. 1181)

Recorded by ALFRED GOLDING

Voice ♩ = 100
Drum ♩ = 100
Drum-rhythm similar to No. 12

Such is my life in this wonderful air, and I long to have little children, a boy and a girl, to enjoy this free air.

Analysis.—This melody is a contrast to the song next preceding, although the subject is the same. A peculiarity common to both is the descending minor third followed by the same interval in ascending progression. There was some uncertainty in the pitch of the low tones transcribed as D sharp and E. These tones were short and always sung distinctly. The tonality is minor and the progressions are very unusual. The most frequent interval is a semitone, comprising one-third of the progressions, and the next in frequency is the major third. The interval of a fourth occurs chiefly between the phrases.

No. 76. The Humming Bird Speaks

(Catalogue No. 1182)

Recorded by ALFRED GOLDING

FREE TRANSLATION

When the humming bird met the redbird she said that she was nothing but a simple little humming bird.

She said that she tried to enjoy things the same as the redbird, and that she also had been wishing to have some little children, so they could enjoy the free air and the liberty of which the redbird had spoken.

Analysis.—In this melody we find the simplicity mentioned in the words but not the rapidity of the humming bird's motion. The song contains both long and short phrases and has no rhythmic unit. The fourth is raised a semitone in every occurrence but is not an important tone. Progression is chiefly by whole tones. (Cf. No. 14.)

No. 77. The Owl Hooted

(Catalogue No. 1183)

Recorded by ALFRED GOLDING

Voice ♩ = 108
Drum ♩ = 108
Drum - rhythm similar to No. 4

FREE TRANSLATION

The owl was requested to do as much as he knew how. He only hooted and told of the morning star, and hooted again and told of the dawn.

Analysis.—The song of the owl is brief and is characterized by syncopations. It contains no rhythmic unit, and the melody tones are the major triad and sixth. About three-fourths of the intervals are major thirds, occurring about equally in ascending and descending progression.

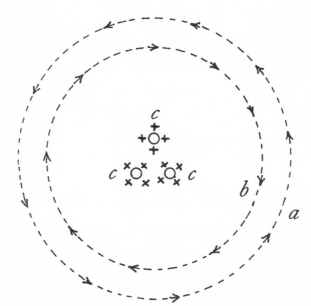

FIGURE 7.—Diagram of Deer dance

No. 78. The Redbird and His Shadow

(Catalogue No. 1184)

Recorded by ALFRED GOLDING

Voice ♩ = 96
Drum ♩ = 96
Drum - rhythm similar to No. 12

FREE TRANSLATION

The redbird takes his shadow with him and is standing at the farther end, well prepared to watch the dancing.

Analysis.—A descending trend within a compass of two measures is an interesting characteristic of this song, together with a large proportion of descending major thirds. The rhythmic unit is short and unimportant. With the exception of two half notes the melody contains only quarter and eighth notes. Although the song is analyzed with D flat as its keynote, the framework of the melody consists of the minor triad and minor seventh in B flat. This is a framework occasionally found in Indian songs and in other primitive music. (Cf. Bull. 45, p. 130, footnote; also Bull. 53, p. 258.)

In the song next following in the series (not transcribed) the redbird tells of his dreams and says, " This will be my kind of dancing and singing, and it shall so be danced."

No. 79. Song of the Nighthawk (a)

(Catalogue No. 1185)

Recorded by ALFRED GOLDING

Voice ♩ = 96
Drum ♩ = 96
Drum - rhythm similar to No. 12

FREE TRANSLATION

The redbird requested the nighthawk to sing, and here he is singing and telling of the morning. He did not dance.

Analysis.—This is the first of a group of four songs of the nighthawk, all of which are minor in tonality. This is a darting melody, with alternate descent and ascent of intervals, and at the close, a flutter of whole-tone progressions. It is minor in tonality and lacks the fourth and seventh tones of the complete octave. Two rhythmic units occur and are entirely different in character. Almost half the intervals are whole tones and 20 per cent of the intervals are fourths.

No. 80. Song of the Nighthawk (b)

(Catalogue No. 1186)

Recorded by ALFRED GOLDING

Voice ♩ = 92
Drum ♩ = 92
Drum-rhythm similar to No. 12

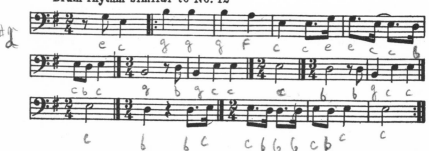

The nighthawk is telling of his dreams and of the power that is given him from his manner of life.

Analysis.—In this song of the nighthawk we have one of the most pleasing melodies in the entire series. It is simple and graceful, and each phrase has a completeness which is unusual. All the phrases end with a descending progression except the last, which ends with an ascending whole tone. The song is minor in tonality and is based on the second 5-toned scale.

No. 81. Song of the Nighthawk (c)

(Catalogue No. 1187)

Recorded by ALFRED GOLDING

Voice ♩ = 92
Drum ♩ = 92
Drum-rhythm similar to No. 12

The daylight is coming and I can distinguish objects around me.

Analysis.—The rhythmic unit of this song is a quick, darting phrase. Attention is directed to the fifth and sixth measures which resemble the rhythmic unit but are more steady and emphatic. The progressions are divided with unusual evenness between major and minor thirds and major and minor seconds, the only interval other than these being an ascending fifth. It is interesting to note the persistence with which the sixth is raised a semitone in the latter portion of the song.

No. 82. Song of the Nighthawk (d)

(Catalogue No. 1188)

Recorded by ALFRED GOLDING

Voice ♩ = 92
Drum ♩ = 92
Drum-rhythm similar to No 12

FREE TRANSLATION

Now the sun is up and the nighthawk is enjoying the light and going from one place to another.

Analysis.—Ascending and descending intervals are about equal in this interesting melody. The phrases vary in length and a majority end with an ascending progression, giving an unusual effect. The song contains no rhythmic unit and moves freely in its compass of seven tones. It begins and ends on the keynote, a portion of the melody lying above and a portion below the keynote.

YAQUI DEER DANCE

The Yaqui village of Guadalupe, near Phoenix, Ariz. (see p. 16), was visited almost daily during the week that preceded Easter, 1922, and the native celebration of holy week was witnessed. The form of the celebration differed from that seen by the writer in the Yaqui village near Tucson the previous year. At that time the accompaniment consisted of drums and reed instruments resembling " shepherd's pipes." The musical instruments used at Guadalupe were more varied and included violins. In both villages the performance was a strange mixture of Roman Catholicism, paganism, and individual originality. The music in both was extremely rhythmic, and especially at Tucson, where it was continued day and night, it showed a quality which might develop into a frenzy or fanatic abandon among the people.

On the day before Easter at Guadalupe a performance was enacted
which may briefly be described as a religious procession or pageant,
in which the Deer dance was an important feature. The procession
started about 200 feet from the entrance of an outdoor chapel
(ramada) in which an altar was placed. The Deer dancers were
stationed about one-third the distance from the entrance, in the path
of the procession, and near them was a group of men with violins.
The performances of these two groups of men were interpolated
with the songs of the religious procession. The Deer dance was
danced intermittently from noon until midnight. It was said that in
old times it was danced at night only, and that in the morning two
or three men went out to hunt deer, but the dance does not appear to
have been held in order to insure success in this hunt. The native
name is Dacio, meaning deer, though it is sometimes called the Ante-
lope dance. The dance usually began about 8 or 9 o'clock, each portion of the night having its proper songs and those preceding No. 89
were sung before midnight. The entire number of dancers was
usually from four to six, with four singers playing on the instruments
to be described. In the dance witnessed by the writer there were four
dancers and four singers.

The musical instruments played by the singers comprised four
halves of very large gourds, disposed as follows: One was inverted
on the water in a tub and struck with a small stick, another was
inverted on the ground and similarly struck, and the other two were
used as resonators for small sets of rasping sticks, one stick being
notched and resting on the gourd, while the other was moved per-
pendicularly across the notches. The beat of the sticks on the
gourds was steady and there was an even rhythm in the friction of
the rasping sticks. One of the half gourds used at this dance was
obtained, together with a set of the rasping sticks. (Pl. 28.) Two
dancers carried rattles made of a flat piece of wood about 6 inches
long, within which were set two pairs of tin disks. (Pl. 29, a.)

The costumes of the four dancers were scanty, nothing being worn
above the waist. The leader, who danced alone much of the time,
wore a pair of small deer horns fastened to the top of his head. The
other three dancers had no headgear except small, rather heavy
wooden masks which were tied with cords in such a manner that the
dancer could push the mask to the side of his head when not dancing. The masks were human faces painted grotesquely and had
stiff hair set in slits of the wood to represent eyebrows. A special
rattle was worn by the leading dancer. This consisted of cocoons
sewn together side by side, forming a strip 6 or 8 feet long which
was wound around the dancer's leg below the knee. Each cocoon
contained a few small pebbles which gave forth a soft, jingling

sound with his motion. The rattle worn on this occasion was said to be very old and above any valuation in money. A similar ornament, collected in 1870 by Dr. Edward L. Palmer, is shown in Plate 29, *b*, and is recorded at the United States National Museum as "used in the Poscola dance." The cocoons were identified as *Rothschildia jorulla.*

A portion of the Deer dance songs was recorded by Juan Ariwares (pl. 30, *a*), who led the dance witnessed in 1922. The recording was done on the day after Easter. (See p. 22.) Ariwares said that he knew the entire series, which would require a whole night for its performance. It was with some difficulty that he selected the songs here presented, selecting some from those used during each part of the night.

It was said that in the following song the people call upon the deer while dancing.

No. 83. Dancing Song

(Catalogue No. 1273)

Recorded by JUAN ARIWARES

Analysis.—All the songs of the Deer dance were recorded without accompaniment, the usual manner of accompaniment being noted in the description of the songs and dance. This song, which is typical of a portion of the series, contains many short notes and a descending trend in brief sections of the melody, followed by a return to a higher note. The intonation was wavering, which may be attributed to several causes. The intervals are small. The singer was an old man, and it was difficult for him to sing alone, without accompaniment. The rapid tones were given with distinctness, but the words could not be transcribed. The language of all these songs is obsolete, but the meaning is known to singers at the Deer dance, who are the only persons having the right to sing the songs.

The song next recorded was not transcribed, as it so closely resembled the dancing song. The words were said to mean, "The wind is moving the yellow flowers," referring to the flowers on certain bushes in Mexico, the flowers being called ai'aiya.

a. JUAN ARIWARES (YAQUI)

b. MIKE BARLEY (COCOPA)

a. ALFRED GOLDING (YUMA)

b. MRS. CHARLES WILSON (YUMA)

No. 84. The Quail in the Bush

(Catalogue No. 1274)

Recorded by JUAN ARIWARES

FREE TRANSLATION

The quail in the bush is making his sound (whirring).

Analysis.—The intonation and time values in this song were excellent.— A majority of the phrases consist of two or three measures, but the succession of seven measures at the close of the first portion of the song was sung without a breathing space. More than two-thirds of the progressions are whole tones. As in several other Yaqui songs of the Deer dance, there was a pause of about two and a half counts before the repeated portion and between the renditions of the song. A longer rest, occurring after the repeated portion, is indicated as " pause ad lib." Other Yaqui songs with the same range are Nos. 88, 89, 91, 93, and 95.

No. 85. The Little Fly

(Catalogue No. 1275)

Recorded by JUAN ARIWARES

FREE TRANSLATION

Brother Little Fly flies around and looks at the sun.

Analysis.—It is interesting to note that this song is concerning a little fly and that 17 of the 20 progressions are whole tones. The song has a compass of five tones and contains all the tones within that compass. The manner of singing this song was especially clear-cut, each tone being given with distinctness. A downward trend is evident throughout the melody.

No. 86. Voices of the People

(Catalogue No. 1276)

Recorded by JUAN ARIWARES

FREE TRANSLATION

The people are talking and calling to each other.

Analysis.—Each phrase in this song has a descending trend. The song is harmonic in structure, which is somewhat unusual in the Deer dance songs. More than half the intervals are whole tones, the interval next in frequency being a minor third, although the song is major in tonality.

No. 87. The Deer Are At Play

(Catalogue No. 1277)

Recorded by JUAN ARIWARES

FREE TRANSLATION

Away in the brush they (the deer) are playing.

Analysis.—The character of this melody is playful in accordance with the words. The first 13 measures were sung four times, these renditions being separated by a break in the time, which varied from approximately two to four counts. The ascending major sixth in the seventh measure is interesting, as well as the triple measure that follows it. The song has a compass of an octave and is based on the fourth 5-toned scale. Almost half the intervals are in descending progression.

No. 88. The Deer and the Flower

(Catalogue No. 1278)

Recorded by JUAN ARIWARES

FREE TRANSLATION

The deer looks at a flower.

Analysis.—The first performance of this song comprised three renditions of the repeated portion with a break in the time between each. The latter part of the song followed after a brief pause. The melody contains little interest, and it is noted that the idea expressed in the words is simple. The song has a range of five tones and contains the major triad and second. More than half the intervals are whole tones and occur only in descending progression.

The following songs were sung after midnight:

No. 89. The Summer Rains

(Catalogue No. 1279)

Recorded by JUAN ARIWARES

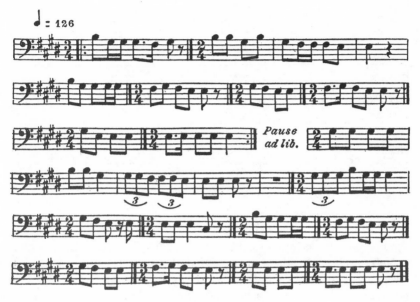

FREE TRANSLATION

In summer the rains come and the grass comes up.
That is the time that the deer has new horns.

Analysis.—Although rhythmic in character this song contains no rhythmic unit. The first portion was sung three times with a break in the time between the repetitions. The intonation on the repetitions of a tone was not steadily held, the pitch being lower on the last tones of the series.

No. 90. The Rising Sun

(Catalogue No. 1280)

Recorded by JUAN ARIWARES

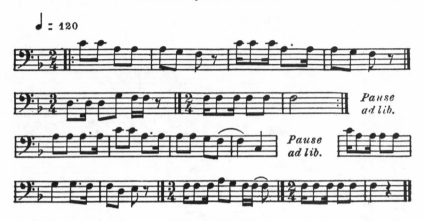

FREE TRANSLATION

The sun is coming up.
It is the time to go out and see the clouds.

Analysis.—Two intervals give character to this rather monotonous melody. These are the ascending fourth in the fourth measure followed by a descending interval and the descending minor third in the fourth from the last measure followed by an ascending interval. The melody consists of short phrases each with a downward trend but with no rhythmic unit. The melody tones are those of the fourth 5-toned scale.

The word "singing" in the next song refers to the putting forth of magic power.

No. 91. The Bush is Singing

(Catalogue No. 1281)

Recorded by JUAN ARIWARES

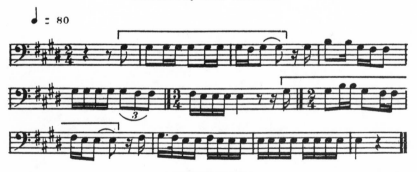

FREE TRANSLATION

The bush is sitting under the tree and singing.

Analysis.—This song is slow in tempo and almost recitative in style. Perhaps the repeated sixteenth notes were suggested by the motion of the leaves of the little bush. The song is in four periods, a unit of rhythm occurring in the first and third period. The tone material is the major triad and second, and 14 of the 19 progressions are whole tones.

No. 92. The Hunt (a)

(Catalogue No. 1282)

Recorded by JUAN ARIWARES

FREE TRANSLATION

The man riding a horse is coming after the deer.

Analysis.—The time was not strictly maintained in this song and a long recitative phrase in the final rendition is not transcribed. This took the place of the seven measures which begin the last half of the song, and was followed by the quarter rest and final measures as transcribed. The style of the entire melody suggests a narrative which is sung instead of spoken, and yet the accents were clearly given. The phrases are short and there is no rhythmic unit. The song contains 41 progressions, 28 of which are whole tones and 12 are semitones.

No. 93. The Hunt (b)

(Catalogue No. 1283)

Recorded by JUAN ARIWARES

FREE TRANSLATION

The man is going to hunt the deer.
They said the sun was coming out and this day they would have the deer.

Analysis.—The small compass of this song is the same as in several other songs of the series. (See No. 84.) It will be noted that the portion of this song between the two pauses is almost identical with the portion preceding the first pause. The differences, however, were steadily maintained in the several renditions. The 5–8 measure and the recitative style in the latter portion are of unusual interest, the repeated sixteenth notes at the end of the song growing softer until they trail away into silence. More than half the progressions are whole tones and the ascending and descending intervals are about equal in number.

No. 94. The Hunt (c)

(Catalogue No. 1284)

Recorded by JUAN ARIWARES

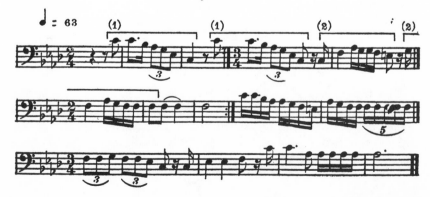

A man said he would surely get the deer and hang it on a tree.

Analysis.—The compass of this song is an octave and the two opening phrases each contain a descent from the highest to the lowest tone. The repeated portion was sung three times without a break in the time and the tone transcribed as E natural was clearly given in all the renditions. The tempo was slightly retarded in the two closing measures. Progression is chiefly by small intervals, 16 of the 38 intervals being whole tones and 7 being semitones.

The next is the final song of the dance.

No. 95. The Deer is Dancing

(Catalogue No. 1285)

Recorded by JUAN ARIWARES

FREE TRANSLATION

The deer is coming out (meaning that the deer is dancing in the middle of the circle).

Analysis.—An effect of vigor and briskness is given to this melody by the phrases with sixteenth notes occurring in the second and sixth measures. The song begins and ends on the same tone and has the same compass and tone material as several others of the present series. (See No. 84.) The portion of the song preceding the double bar was sung four times with a slight break in the time between the renditions. After a brief pause the connective phrase was sung and followed by the repeated portion without a break in the time. This appears to constitute a complete performance.

MAYO DEER DANCE

The Deer dance is held by the Mayo as well as by the Yaqui and Yuma. A Mayo song was sung by the singer of the Yaqui Deer dance songs, who said he considered it particularly good. It was sung in the latter part of the night. The meaning of the words of the song is not known.

No. 96. Song of the Deer Dance

(Catalogue No. 1292)

Recorded by JUAN ARIWARES

Analysis.—The tone A occurs frequently in this song, being sung A natural in the first portion and A flat in the second portion of the melody. This change causes the song to be classified as both major and minor in tonality. The song has a compass of five tones and uses all the tones within that compass. There is no change of measure lengths and the melody progresses chiefly by whole tones.

YUMA CA'KORAMU'S DANCE

Five songs of this old dance were recorded by Katcora, but only two were transcribed. They are part of a cycle which required one night for its rendition and was said to be " about the stars in the sky." The words were in a language that is obsolete, but their meaning was known to the singer, who said the first song of the entire series was about the evening. Another song mentioned " the Pleiades and three stars in a row," and another was concerning Coyote, who laughed at the dancers. These songs were not transcribed. The subjects of the other songs are indicated by their titles. The song concerning the meadow lark and the diver " would be sung along toward morning." The people could not understand the words of these songs, and it was customary for the singer after completing a song to announce its subject. Thus after this song he would say to the people, " I have sung about the meadow lark and the diver." The songs in the early part of the evening were always sung softly, the singing growing gradually louder as the series progressed.

From the songs and the description of the dance, as given by Katcora, this appears to have been a dance of the " Pleiades " type.[32] The dancers were described as wearing paint and feathers. They stood in their places and the dance motion consisted of "bending the knees and stooping low." The singer faced the east, according to the custom in Yuma dances.

No. 97. Song Concerning the Meadow Lark and the Diver

(Catalogue No. 1236)

Recorded by KATCORA

[32] Dances of the "Pleiades" type stand apart from all others as being primarily dance singings. They are connected with two long myths. "The Pleiades singer stands under a shade with his back to the sun. Behind him young men stand abreast, and behind these their elders. They wear feather-hung rabbit-skin ropes over their shoulders. Facing the singer are a row of girls and one of older women. All sing with him for a time. Then he ceases, but they continue to dance. They bend and raise the body, make a long stride forward with the right knee elevated, bend again, and step back. As the men step backward, the women step forward, and vice versa." (Kroeber, Handbook of the Indians of California, Bull. 78, Bur. Amer. Ethn., pp. 764–765.)

Analysis.—This is a particularly fluent melody and contains 98 progressions in 23 measures. The song is minor in tonality, but only 10 progressions are minor thirds, the whole tone comprising about 60 per cent and the major third about 23 per cent of the intervals. The tempo is slow and the tones are those of the second 5-toned scale.

No. 98. Song Concerning the Quail

(Catalogue No. 1237)

Recorded by KATCORA

Voice ♩ = 168
Rattle ♩ = 168
Rattle-rhythm similar to No. 27

Analysis.—This song is characterized by a syncopation which occurs frequently, the rattle being approximately in eighth notes. The song contains the tones of the second 5-toned scale, beginning and ending on the third above the keynote. Progression is chiefly by whole tones, though the fourth is a prominent interval. The repeated portion, as in many Yuma songs, was sung four times.

COCOPA BIRD DANCE

The songs of this and the two dances next following afford an interesting contrast in their general character. The Cocopa songs of the Bird dance were learned by the singer when he was a "helper," but those of the Mohave Bird dance are common property, being known to all the tribe. The songs of the second Cocopa dance (Tcumánpa'xwa) were regarded with respect by the singer, who said he inherited them from his grandfather, who probably received them in a dream. The Bird dance could be held before a cremation or a Memorial ceremony.

Among the Cocopa, whose songs are here presented, this dance is commonly known by the Yuma term " Elca'," meaning little bird. The Cocopa term, with the same meaning, is Esa'elmu's. The Yuma also call the songs Atsiyĕ'r (bird) Scava'rr (song). No explanation of the term was obtained. It was said "because a song mentions birds it is not a regular bird song, as insects are also mentioned in the bird songs. Herzog states that these songs are concerning "a kind of jay bird which lives on piñon nuts and comes to the Diegueño country from the Mexican side." [33]

These songs were recorded by Numa'wàsoà't, a middle-aged member of the Cocopa Tribe. Frank Tehanna traveled many miles on horseback to explain the writer's work to Numawàsoàt, who was considered a particularly good singer. He speaks no English and at first he hesitated to record the songs, but his objections were overcome by Tehanna and he came to the Cocopa village to record the songs. Numa'wàsoà't learned the songs in the usual manner, by being one of the "helpers." He has acted as leader of the singers at the dance, being seated and usually having two helpers at each side. He and each of his helpers had a gourd rattle. The dancers were young women, from one to five in number. They stood in a row facing the singers, and when dancing they moved backward and forward a distance of about 15 feet. The Bird dance lasted all night, and the songs were in regular sequence, certain songs being sung before and after midnight. The singer selected a few from each part of the series and all the records were studied, though only a portion were transcribed. Several songs were almost monotones and others consisted chiefly of ascending and descending minor thirds. The songs that were sung in the early portion of the night were always begun softly and gradually increased in volume of tone. The words are in the "old language," which is not understood by anyone at the present time. The songs were recorded with the rattle shown in Plate 23.

---

[33] Herzog, Yuman Musical Style, Jour. Amer. Folk-Lore, vol. 41, footnote p. 187.

No. 99. Opening Song of the Dance

(Catalogue No. 1243)

Recorded by NUMAWÁSOÀT

Voice ♩ = 96
Rattle ♩ = 96
See rattle-rhythm below

Rattle-rhythm

Analysis.—The only tones occurring in this song are D, F, and G, and the ascending intervals are more in number than the descending. The intervals which impress the ear most strongly are the ascending minor third and the descending fourth. The melody is particularly cheerful, with an interesting rhythmic unit, the third measure of which appears in the portion of the song not containing the entire unit. The rhythm of the rattle could not be heard in all the renditions, and the rattle was silent during the pause and the measures immediately following the pause.

No. 100. Song in the Early Evening (a)

(Catalogue No. 1244)

Recorded by NUMAWÁSOÁT

Voice ♩ = 92
Rattle ♩ = 92
See rattle - rhythm below

Rattle when discernible

Analysis.—An unusual number of semitones occurs in this song and is its chief characteristic. Almost half the intervals are semitones, 11 occurring in ascending and 12 in descending progression. A whole tone occurs only once. The song is minor in tonality and contains all the tones of the octave except the sixth and seventh. The rhythm is not so simple as in the preceding song. It is interesting to note the rhythm in the portion following the pause. In these measures a triplet is accented and a sixteenth note followed by an eighth appears on the unaccented count, reversing the order in the earlier portion of the song. The coincidence of rattle and voice was exact in counts having the same division.

No. 101. Song in the Early Evening (b)

(Catalogue No. 1245)

Recorded by Numawásoat

Voice ♩ = 96
Rattle ♩ = 96
Rattle-rhythm similar to No. 99

Analysis.—This song begins and ends on the same tone, a melodic formation not so common in Cocopa as in the analyzed Yuma songs. Like the song next preceding, this begins with an ascending fifth, followed by a descending whole tone, but the other characteristics of the song are different. This song is based on the fourth 5-toned scale and has a compass of seven tones. The principal interval is the minor third which comprises about half the progressions. The phrase indicated as a rhythmic unit is five measures in length and its repetitions comprise almost the entire song. The rattle was clearly discernible throughout the performance.

No. 102. Song in the Early Evening (c)

(Catalogue No. 1246)

Recorded by NUMAWÁSOÁT

Voice ♩ = 96
Rattle ♩ = 96
Rattle-rhythm similar to No. 99

Analysis.—It is interesting to note the " answering " of the successive phrases in this song, suggesting an advance and receding by the dancers. The rhythmic unit is short and simple, beginning alternately with a descending and an ascending progression. The minor third constitutes about half the progressions in the song, which is major in tonality and based on the fourth 5-toned scale.

No. 103. Song at About Midnight (a)

(Catalogue No. 1247)

Recorded by NUMAWÀSOÀT

Analysis.—Three interesting peculiarities appear in this song, all being given with distinctness. The first is the syncopation, which occurs in the opening measure and several times during the song; the second is the accidental, occurring only in a short, detached phrase; and the third is the frequency of short rests, giving crispness to the melody. The most frequent intervals are fourths and minor thirds, the former comprising 20 and the latter 23 of the 70 progressions. The ascending intervals are more in number than the descending intervals. This has been noted with some frequency in Yuma and Cocopa songs, but occurs seldom in the songs previously analyzed.

No. 104. Song at About Midnight (b)

(Catalogue No. 1248)

Recorded by NUMAWÁSOÁT

Voice ♩ = 108

Analysis.—Like the preceding song, this has a compass of seven tones, is based on the fourth 5-toned scale, and has the sixth lowered a semitone. Unlike the preceding, it contains no rhythmic unit, though the several phrases bear a close resemblance to one another. The ascending and descending intervals are about equal in number. About 57 per cent of the intervals are minor thirds, although the song is major in tonality.

No. 105. Song at About Midnight (c)

(Catalogue No. 1249)

Recorded by NUMAWÁSOÁT

Analysis.—Two measures transcribed in quadruple time occur in this melody and are unusual in recorded Indian songs. There were no secondary accents in these measures which appear to serve as an introduction to the rhythmic unit. The rattle was somewhat irregular in the quadruple measures and was continuous during the pause of the voice. The song progresses chiefly by whole tones which comprise about two-thirds of the intervals.

No. 106. Song at About Midnight (d)

(Catalogue No. 1250)

Recorded by NUMAWÀSOÀT

Analysis.—This song contains a particularly clear thematic form. Three rhythmic units occur, and the contrasts between them are interesting. The first unit contains a descending minor third and the second contains an ascending minor third, while the third unit contains this interval in both ascending and descending progression.

The two measures following the pause contain a descending trend, followed by three measures which resemble all the rhythmic units without duplicating any of them. About three-fourths of the intervals are minor thirds, this interval occurring 32 times in ascending and 33 times in descending progression. The melody tones are those of the fourth 5-toned scale.

No. 107. Song Concerning the Diver

(Catalogue No. 1251)

Recorded by NUMAWĂSOĂT

Rattle when discernable

Analysis.—In this and the four songs next following the fourth is a prominent interval. All these songs were sung in the early morning. Three of the series are based on the fourth 5-toned scale. The present song is major in tonality, but the interval of a major third does not occur. More than half the 62 intervals are minor thirds and 22 are fourths. Attention is directed to the note values in measures 14 to 16, which were given with distinctness.

No. 108. Song Concerning the Pleiades

(Catalogue No. 1252)

Recorded by NUMAWÁSOÁT

Analysis.—Songs concerning a star appear to be unusual among the Indians. A Chippewa song for success in hunting contained the words, " Like a star I shine, the animal, gazing, is fascinated by my light." (Bull. 45, No. 69.) A song of the Midewiwin in the same tribe contained the words " Beautiful as a star hanging in the sky is our Mide lodge." (Bull. 45, No. 44.) Two Pawnee songs mentioned a star which spoke in a dream and gave assistance. (Bull. 93, Nos. 57 and 80.) The present melody is characterized by an accented high tone, slightly prolonged and followed by a descending trend of six or seven tones. The compass is seven tones, which occurs frequently in the present series. Progression is chiefly by minor thirds, but the descending fourth is a frequent and prominent interval.

No. 109. Song in the Early Morning (a)

(Catalogue No. 1253)

Recorded by NUMAWASOAT

Rattle, when discernible

Analysis.—In this song a semitone constitutes about one-third of the progressions. This interval appears to be difficult for an Indian to sing. It occurs infrequently in recorded Indian songs (see Tables 11 and 12, pp. 33 and 205), and its transcription should be understood as approximate in pitch. The intonation on the tone transcribed as E was also uncertain, this tone frequently being sung lower than the indicated pitch. Two rhythmic units occur, the second reversing the principal count division of the first unit. The song is analyzed with G sharp as its keynote, but the corresponding key is not established in the melody. This song was recorded also by Katcora, the melody being the same.

No. 110. Song in the Early Morning (b)

(Catalogue No. 1254)

Recorded by NUMAWÁSOÀT

Analysis.—The phrases in this song are unusually short and the rhythmic unit contains only four tones. The melody is based on the fourth 5-toned scale, but the keynote of that series occurs only twice and the principal interval is the minor third. The rhythm of the rattle was descernible throughout the performance and its rhythm conforms to that of the melody except in the opening measures, during which it was shaken rapidly. The term " tremolo " is sometimes used to designate this rapid motion of the rattle.

No. 111. Closing Song of the Dance

(Catalogue No. 1255)

Recorded by Numawásoàt

Analysis.—No change of measure length occurs in this song which is in 5–8 time. Both these peculiarities are unusual in recorded Indian songs. (See Tables 15 and 16, pp. 35 and 206.) A further peculiarity is the ending on the tone above the keynote. The song is based on the triad F, A, C, but G appears twice as an accented tone and is also the closing tone. Attention is directed to the occurrence of a sixteenth note as an accented tone and also as an unaccented tone following instead of preceding a dotted eighth note. The accents were strongly given in all renditions.

MOHAVE BIRD DANCE

It was said that the songs of this dance were particularly pleasing, but only four were recorded, as the Mohave songs were not a subject of special investigation. Three were transcribed and show a somewhat different structure than the Yuman and Cocopa. These Mohave songs have a somewhat larger compass and are more lively in general character than the songs of the other Yuman tribes under consideration. Leonard Cleveland, who recorded the songs, is an educated Mohave, living on the Yuma Reservation.

Each portion of the night had its own songs in this as in other song cycles and the songs here presented were sung about midnight. The words of the first song were concerning the darkness and the words of the second song (not transcribed) were concerning a certain sort of birds " on their way traveling up north."

No. 112. Bird Dance Song (a)

(Catalogue No. 1289)

Recorded by LEONARD CLEVELAND

Analysis.—Two rhythmic units occur in this song, differing only in the divisions of one count. In the middle portion of the song the group of four sixteenth notes is transferred from the unaccented count to the accented count, giving variety and character to the rhythm of the song as a whole. The compass is nine tones, the only songs in this work which have a compass of more than an octave being this and No. 124, which has a compass of 10 tones. The compass of this group of songs is smaller than any previously analyzed, 90 per cent having a range of seven tones or less. (See Table 5, p. 30.) Among the Papago songs the highest percentage had a compass of an octave, these comprising 40 per cent of the entire number. (Bull. 89, Table 5, p. 6.) The highest percentage of songs with a large compass were found among the Chippewa, 41 per cent having a compass of 12 or more tones, but the largest compass was found among the Sioux, three songs of that tribe having a compass of 17 tones. (Bull. 61, Table 5A, p. 28.) About half the progressions in this song are whole tones. The fourth is a prominent interval in ascending progressions.

In the next song the birds speak, saying, "Now we are gone."

No. 113. Bird Dance Song (b)

(Catalogue No. 1290)

Recorded by LEONARD CLEVELAND

Analysis.—No other song recorded by the writer has contained the alternating phrases in different tempi which characterize this song. The phrases are indicated as the rhythmic units and one contains a rest. These phrases or units are different in character as well as in tempo, the first containing two triplets and the second containing two dotted eighth notes. Minor thirds and major seconds are about equal in number and together constitute 33 of the 39 intervals in the song.

Concerning the final song it was said: "The birds stop now to eat and see some cattle. They say this in the song."

No. 114. Bird Dance Song (c)

(Catalogue No. 1291)

Recorded by LEONARD CLEVELAND

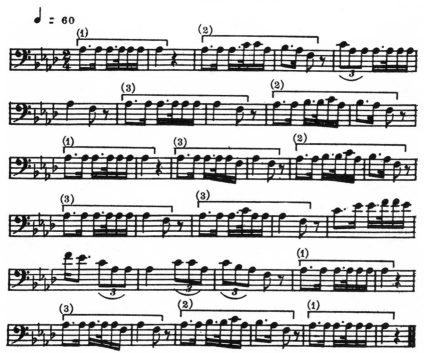

Analysis.—Three rhythmic units occur in this song, each containing two measures and differing from the others in the count divisions of the second measure. The melody contains little variety except in the portion which ascends to E flat and F, this being an unusually interesting and pleasing phrase. The whole tone is the most frequent progression, comprising 24 of the 60 intervals. The song has a compass of eight tones and is based on the second 5-toned scale.

COCOPA TCUMÁNPA'XWA DANCE

The meaning of the name of this dance was not ascertained. It was danced by unmarried girls and men, usually five to seven in number. There were more singers than in the Bird dance, the leader often having three or four helpers on either side, each man having a gourd rattle. At first they were all seated, the singers in a row and the dancers facing them. When all was ready they sprang to their feet, the singers advancing and pushing the line of dancers backward. The distance thus traversed was according to the wish of the singers, perhaps a few feet or perhaps quite a distance. Sometimes the lines were 3 feet apart and sometimes only about a foot apart. In its motion the dance resembles the Bear dance of the Northern Ute, as described in Bulletin 75, pages 57–58.

The step of this dance was about 4 inches, or even less, in length, the foot which was moved backward being placed on the ground with the toe scarcely halfway down the ball of the other foot. With each step the knees were bent and the head thrust slightly forward. It was said that " they moved backward, then forward, then stopped and danced standing still."

The songs of this dance were recorded by a young man commonly known as Mike Barley (pl. 30, b), who spoke no English and hesitated to sing the songs in the daytime. He said that he inherited them from his grandfather and could sing them without being taught, this being in accord with the Yuman belief that a man may " dream " the knowledge of song cycles. The entire series of songs required an entire night for rendition, and there was said to be no narrative in it, the series being only for dancing. Each part of the night had its own songs, but the singer selected a few from those which were sung " along toward morning." The words were in the " old language." The first songs of the dance were said to mention the evening and certain animals and insects, but beyond this the meaning of the songs was not known.

One of the records made by Mike Barley was played for Katcora, a Yuma singer and informant, who repeated the syllables (or words), but said he did not know the meaning. He also recorded the song, his rendition being practically a duplicate of the one here presented.

No. 115. Dancing Song (a)

(Catalogue No. 1268)

♩ = 84   Recorded by MIKE BARLEY

Rattle

Analysis.—This and the four songs next following are songs of a different dance than the Bird dance and the general character is different. They are more spirited and the rhythm is more decided. A persistent accent on a high tone followed by a descending and then an ascending trend is a characteristic of the present song. Attention is directed to the quadruple measures which, with a slightly prolonged rest, serve to break the steady swing of the rhythm. After the pause we find a reversal of a previous count division in which a sixteenth note is accented, while the dotted eighth follows on the unaccented part of the count. The rhythm of the rattle is continuous except during the long pause. The only intervals are major and minor thirds and whole tones. The song, which is so energetic, has a compass of only five tones.

No. 116. Dancing Song (b)

(Catalogue No. 1269)

Recorded by MIKE BARLEY

No. 116 (continued)

Analysis.—This song contains only the tones F, A flat, B flat, and C flat, the latter being given with distinctness. This is an example of a melody which is not in accordance with an established system. These tones might be used in such a sequence as to suggest A flat as the keynote, but F is so strongly emphasized and so closely associated with A flat that the song is analyzed as being in the key of F minor with the fifth lowered a semitone. This should be recognized as one of the instances in which ordinary musical notation and the present system of analysis are used only to assist observation of the melody. Two rhythmic units occur, the difference between them being chiefly in the accent on the three dotted eighth notes, this group being unaccented in the first unit and strongly accented in the second unit.

No. 117. Dancing Song (c)

(Catalogue No. 1270)

Recorded by MIKE BARLEY

Analysis.—This song has a compass of four tones, but uses only the first, third, and fourth of these tones. The difference between the two rhythmic units was slight but steadily maintained. The rattle was particularly clear and its correlation with the voice on the triplets was not exact but the transcription is near enough for practical purposes. As in No. 105, the rattle was continuous during the pause of the voice. The rendition closed with a repetition of the last twelve measures.

No. 118. Dancing Song (d)

(Catalogue No. 1271)

Recorded by MIKE BARLEY

Analysis.—This song has a compass of six tones, using all the tones in the compass except the second. The tonality is minor, but the major third comprises 18 of the 65 intervals. The intonation in the latter part of the song was uncertain on the tone A, and the transcription of the measures containing D sharp and A sharp should be regarded as approximate. Attention is directed to the syncopation, followed by a descending trend and an ascent to the original tone, this melodic movement suggesting the forward and backward motion of the dancers. The final interval is descending, in contrast to many songs of this series which close with an ascending progression.

No. 119. Dancing Song (e)

(Catalogue No. 1272)

Recorded by MIKE BARLEY

Analysis.—This song is somewhat monotonous in its melodic trend but the rhythm is energetic and interesting. As in many of these songs, the highest tones occur in the measures immediately following the pause. A syncopation occurs, also several quadruple measures. The melodic tones are those of the major triad and second. The intervals comprise only major and minor thirds and major seconds, the latter constituting two-thirds of the progressions. The general rhythm and the rhythmic unit resemble those of other songs of this dance.

YUMA TUNA'K DANCE

It was the early custom of the Yuma to hold a "maturity dance" (Tuna'k) for several girls at a time. A circular hole was dug about 2½ or 3 feet in depth and the girls lay face downward in this hole with their heads toward the south. The dancers were on the edge of this cavity.

The first song of the group is the beginning of the series sung in the evening and says the girls are being placed in the hole. The dance continued all night. Mrs. Wilson (pl. 31, *b*), who recorded the songs, is the wife of Charles Wilson. Her Yuma name is Mavě', said to be a clan name meaning "snake." In addition to the songs she recorded a series of numbers in the "old language" from 1 to 38, saying this was all she could remember of that language.

No. 120. Song of Tunak Dance (a)

(Catalogue No. 1224)

Recorded by Mrs. WILSON

Analysis.—With one exception the only tones in the melody are G sharp, A sharp, and B. A short rhythmic phrase is repeated, and the song as a whole has a rhythmic unity which is interesting and pleasing to the ear. More than half the intervals are semitones.

No. 121. Song of Tunak Dance (b)

(Catalogue No. 1225)

Recorded by Mrs. WILSON

Analysis.—This song is classified as irregular in tonality. With the exception of three intervals the melody progresses by whole tones. The tempo is unusually slow.

No. 122. Song of Tunak Dance (c)

(Catalogue No. 1226)

Recorded by Mrs. WILSON

Analysis.—The compass of this song is only three tones and the progressions consist of 28 whole tones and one ascending major third. Instead of the monotony which might be expected from the progressions we find a varied and pleasing melody due to the rhythm. Attention is directed to the difference in the length of measures 5 and 10 which follow the rhythmic units, the latter of these measures carrying the rhythm forward to the end of the song.

No. 123. Song of Tunak Dance (d)

(Catalogue No. 1227)

Recorded by Mrs. WILSON

Analysis.—The only tones in this melody are G sharp and B, the former being considered the keynote. In rhythm the song is less simple than in its melodic progressions. The eighth note followed by two sixteenth notes can scarcely be considered a rhythmic unit as it occurs on both accented and unaccented counts and forms a part of longer phrases.

YUMA GAMES

The three games played by the Yuma were Tcata's (shinny), Otu'r, a form of "hoop and stick" game, and Peo'n, which consisted in hiding a small object in the hand. The first of these games is described in connection with a man's name, on page 43. The implements of Otur consisted of two poles about 15 feet long, the thickness of a man's thumb, and a hoop 4 to 6 inches in diameter, wound with twine or rags. One player rolled the hoop along the ground, and both players ran after it, throwing their poles toward the hoop. Dr. H. F. C. ten Kate, jr., who witnessed this game among the Yuma, states that the men "hastily threw their poles at the ring so that it is stopped." He was not certain whether the sticks had to be thrown through the ring or whether the count depended upon the particular way in which the pole lay beside it.[34] No songs were used with these games.

The peon game is played only at night. In old times the article hidden was a short piece of the leg bone of a crane.[35]

At the present time any small bone is used. Usually there are four players on each side. They start the singing at the proper time. They kneel in two rows facing each other, and "dance" in that position, bending from side to side, rising up and sinking down again. Usually there is a referee appointed by the two sides who holds the wagers and watches the game. Before the play begins he makes a speech, directing the players to hold up the little bones so everyone can see them; then he gives the signal for the play to begin. The player at one end of the row is first to conceal the bone. If the man directly opposite him guesses correctly in which hand he is holding the bone the play passes to the opposite side. If the first man guesses incorrectly, the man at his left hand may guess, and so on to the end of the line. When one point has been made the singing is started by the players on the winning side and taken up by the crowd standing behind them. The referee sings with either side, as he is supposed to be strictly impartial. The spectators, who wager on the game, usually have silver coins in a handkerchief, and jingle it like a rattle. Articles of value as well as coin are wagered, and are waved in the air above the heads of the players. It is required that the referee shall remember the face of every man who makes a wager and the amount of his bet. If a man makes a false claim and receives money in payment of a bet the referee must replace the amount from

---

[34] Culin, Stewart, Games of the North American Indians, Twenty-fourth Ann. Rept. Bur. Amer. Ethn., p. 526. This game is also mentioned in a legend recorded among the Pawnee, in Bull. 93, Bur. Amer. Ethn., p. 99.

[35] A set of these bones was collected among the Mohave by Dr. Edward L. Palmer, the bones being 2⅜ inches long and one-quarter inch in diameter. Doctor Palmer states: "These bones are made of the leg bone of the white crane. Six pieces constitute the set, there being two sides with three pieces on a side, of different lengths. The game is to guess the length of the pieces held in the hands of the players. A very small end protruded through the fingers. As the opposite sides guess, it is an animated game." Continuing, he states that the same bones are used by the Yuma and Cocopa and that the game is to guess in which hand the bones are held. The bones used by one side are white and those used by the other side are black. (Culin, Games of the North American Indians, Twenty-fourth Ann. Rept. Bur. Amer. Ethn., p. 326.)

his personal funds, as he forgot the man's face and paid money to the wrong person.   Before the money is paid to the winners it is spread out and counted in view of the company, to be sure that all the money which was wagered is in the hands of the referee.   The amount of the individual bets is also sorted out " dollar for dollar."   The game does not proceed until this is fully settled.

The Cocopa often challenged the Yuma to this game, naming the place where the game was to be held.

The songs of the peon game are accompanied by a nasal sound made by forcing the breath through the nose by a spasmodic contraction of the chest.   No drum or rattle is used.   The rhythm of the accompaniment is indicated in the transcription.

Two songs were recorded.   These are very old and the words are in an obsolete language.   The singer, Nelson Rainbow, acted as one of the writer's interpreters among the Cocopa, and the cremation of his son is mentioned on page 43.   He is employed as a carpenter and in other capacities at the agency.

No. 124. Game Song (a)

(Catalogue No. 1241)

Recorded by Nelson Rainbow

Accompaniment rhythm

Analysis.—A vigorous rhythmic unit characterizes this song, its repetitions comprising or influencing the entire melody. Attention is directed to the opening measures, to the seventh and eighth measures, and to a corresponding phrase near the close of the song; these measures closely resembling the rhythmic unit. This has a compass of 10 tones, which is larger than any other song under present analysis. (Cf. No. 112.) The ascent of an octave, occurring midway the length of the song, carries the melody to the highest tone of the compass. The lowest tone is reached in six measures and the song ends on the lower tones of the compass.

No. 125. Game Song (b)

(Catalogue No. 1242)

Recorded by NELSON RAINBOW

♩ = 92

Accompaniment similar to No. 124

Analysis.—This song is based on the second 5-toned scale and has a compass of seven tones. The ascending and descending intervals are equal in number and the minor thirds and major seconds are practically equal in ascending and descending progression. This song is rhythmic in character but contains no unit of rhythm. There are phrases that closely resemble each other, and one is reminded that the purpose of the song was to baffle the player's opponents, attempting to guess the location of a hidden object. Attention is directed to the effect produced by the change to triple time in the seventh measure, and to the ascending whole tone in the thirteenth measure, with the interesting effects produced by these features of the melody.

YUMA SONGS FOR CHILDREN

The following simple melodies were recorded by Mrs. Charles Wilson (pl. 31, *b*), a woman of strong character and gentle manner.

No. 126. Lullaby

(Catalogue No. 1228)

Recorded by Mrs. WILSON

TRANSLATION

Sleep, sleep. It will carry you into the land of wonderful dreams, and in your dreams you will see a future day and your future family.

Analysis.—This is one of the most attractive melodies recorded among the Yuma. It contains a larger variety of intervals than is found in a majority of Indian songs, though about two-thirds of the intervals are major thirds. It is interesting to note the ascent and descent of a seventh in the closing phrase.

No. 127. " Why Did You Cry? "

(Catalogue No. 1229)

Recorded by Mrs. WILSON

TRANSLATION

Why did you cry; why did you cry?
Have you stepped on a thorn; have you stepped on a thorn?

Analysis.—The ascending and descending intervals in this song are about equal in number. The melody moves freely within its compass of seven tones, as it contains 37 progressions in 10 measures. In the opening phrases we seem to hear a question which is repeated near the close of the song. About three-fourths of the intervals are whole tones which are used consecutively throughout the melody. The rapid sixteenth notes in the closing measures are probably required by the words addressed to the child.

No. 128. " Sleep, My Baby "

(Catalogue No. 1230)

Recorded by Mrs. WILSON

TRANSLATION

Sleep, my baby; sleep, my son (or my daughter)

Analysis.—In this pleasing melody we find the ascending fourth followed by a descending whole tone which characterized the songs for treating the sick (Nos. 40–43). This was mentioned in the analyses of these songs as a particularly soothing phrase, and it is interesting to find it in a song to induce sleep. The rhythmic unit contains a different group of tones and is somewhat restless in character. Minor thirds and whole tones are about equal in number; the other intervals comprising one semitone and three ascending fourths.

MISCELLANEOUS YAQUI SONGS

The two songs next following are examples of Yaqui songs with Mexican influence. They were always sung with guitar accompaniment and were recorded in that manner, the sound of the guitar being audible throughout the length of the phonograph cylinder. The words of the song are in the exact language of the interpreter and bear an interesting resemblance to a song of the Tule Indians of Panama which is also given in the words of the interpreter. (Music of the Tule Indians of Panama, No. 9, p. 34.)

TULE LOVE SONG

Many pretty flowers, red, blue and yellow,
We say to the girls, "Let us go and walk among the flowers."
The wind comes and sways the flowers,
The girls are like that when they dance.
Some are wide-open, large flowers and some are tiny little flowers.
The birds love the sunshine and the starlight.
The flowers smell sweet.
The girls are sweeter than the flowers.

No. 129. Song of Admiration

(Catalogue No. 1287)

Recorded by ANKA ALVAREZ

TRANSLATION

In Cocori (a town in Mexico) is a young girl whose name is Hesucita.
She is a pretty girl.
Her eyes look like stars.
Her pretty eyes are like stars moving.

Analysis.—The rhythm of this song is complex and of unusual interest. Two rhythmic units occur, each having a series of four quarter notes followed by a dotted quarter and a descent of the voice, but in the first unit the quarter notes are in triple time and in the second unit they are in double time. Variety is given by the eighth rest in the third occurrence of the first unit, taking the place of the downward slur of the voice on the same interval. This is followed by an upward progression similar to that which follows the first occurrence of the second unit and the song closes gracefully with two occurrences of the first unit. The connective phrase resembles the opening of the song but the first measures are in double instead of triple time.

The next song could be sung at any time and was frequently sung by young men on horseback.

No. 130. Yaqui Song

(Catalogue No. 1286)

Recorded by JOSE MARIE UMADA

TRANSLATION

I have no money to go to the ranch.

Analysis.—This song comprises four periods of five measures each. The first two and the last two have rhythmic units which differ only in the first measure. This difference, with the additional quarter note in the fifth measure, gives character to the rhythm of the song as a whole. The song is minor in tonality, has a compass of six tones and contains all the tones of the octave except the seventh. Half of the intervals are semitones. The melody suggests a Mexican influence, though the Indians insisted that it was a Yaqui song. A distinct slurring of the voice occurred between certain tones, as indicated. The other tones were sung with unusual precision of attack and the rests were given their exact time.

MELODIC AND RHYTHMIC ANALYSIS OF SONGS BY SERIAL NUMBERS

MELODIC ANALYSIS

TABLE 1.—TONALITY

	Serial number of songs	Number	Per cent
Major tonality	1, 2, 4, 12, 15, 19, 21, 22, 23, 25, 27, 31, 33, 34, 35, 36, 39, 40, 41, 42, 43, 44, 45, 46, 47, 48, 50, 52, 53, 54, 65, 67, 70, 71, 77, 78, 84, 85, 86, 87, 88, 89, 90, 91, 92, 93, 95, 101, 102, 103, 104, 105, 106, 107, 108, 110, 111, 112, 119, 122, 127, 129.	62	49
Minor tonality	5, 6, 7, 8, 9, 10, 11, 13, 14, 17, 24, 26, 28, 32, 37, 49, 51, 56, 57, 58, 59, 60, 61, 62, 63, 64, 66, 69, 74, 75, 76, 79, 80, 81, 82, 83, 94, 97, 98, 99, 100, 109, 113, 114, 115, 116, 117, 118, 120, 123, 124, 125, 126, 128, 130.	55	42
Major and minor tonality (same keynote).	96	1	
Third above keynote absent	3, 18, 29, 30, 68	5	3
Irregular in tonality	16, 20, 38, 55, 72, 73, 121	7	5
Total		130	

TABLE 2.—FIRST NOTE OF SONG—ITS RELATION TO KEYNOTE

	Serial number of songs	Number	Per cent
Beginning on the—			
Sixth	3, 18, 21, 33, 54	5	4
Fifth	4, 23, 29, 30, 32, 34, 35, 37, 40, 41, 42, 43, 44, 45, 47, 50, 64, 68, 70, 89, 90, 91, 94, 100, 101, 103, 107, 110.	28	21
Fourth	24, 51, 96, 97, 111, 118	6	4
Third	8, 9, 12, 17, 22, 25, 27, 28, 49, 52, 58, 59, 61, 63, 64, 67, 74, 77, 84, 85, 86, 87, 88, 98, 104, 106, 109, 113, 114, 115, 116, 117, 124, 125, 126, 127, 128, 129, 130.	39	30
Second	26, 102, 105	3	2
Keynote	1, 2, 5, 6, 7, 10, 11, 13, 14, 15, 19, 31, 36, 39, 46, 48, 53, 56, 57, 60, 62, 65, 66, 69, 71, 73, 75, 76, 78, 79, 80, 81, 82, 83, 92, 93, 99, 108, 112, 119, 120, 122, 123.	42	33
Irregular in tonality	16, 20, 38, 55, 72, 73, 121	7	5
Total		130	

TABLE 3.—LAST NOTE OF SONG—ITS RELATION TO KEYNOTE

	Serial number of songs	Number	Per cent
Ending on the—			
Fifth	3, 21, 33, 34, 35, 36, 40, 41, 42, 47, 54, 67, 68, 70, 101, 102, 103, 104, 106, 107, 108, 110, 112.	23	18
Third	4, 7, 8, 9, 11, 12, 13, 17, 22, 23, 29, 30, 32, 43, 45, 50, 51, 52, 58, 74, 77, 94, 98, 99, 113, 114, 116, 117, 118, 124, 125.	31	25
Second	111	1	
Keynote	1, 2, 5, 6, 10, 14, 15, 18, 19, 24, 25, 26, 27, 28, 31, 37, 39, 44, 46, 48, 49, 53, 56, 57, 59, 60, 61, 62, 63, 64, 65, 66, 69, 71, 75, 76, 78, 79, 80, 81, 82, 83, 84, 85, 86, 87, 88, 89, 90, 91, 92, 93, 95, 96, 97, 100, 105, 109, 115, 119, 120, 122, 123, 126, 127, 128, 129, 130.	68	50
Irregular in tonality	16, 20, 38, 55, 72, 73, 121	7	5
Total		130	

TABLE 4.—LAST NOTE OF SONG—ITS RELATION TO COMPASS OF SONG

	Serial number of songs	Number	Per cent.
Songs in which final note is—			
Lowest in song	1, 3, 4, 5, 15, 16, 17, 20, 24, 25, 27, 29, 30, 37, 38, 43, 49, 51, 52, 53, 57, 71, 83, 84, 85, 88, 89, 91, 93, 95, 96, 97, 105, 112, 119, 122, 123, 126, 128.	39	30
Immediately preceded by [1]—			
Fourth below	6, 28, 39, 48, 68, 70, 100, 109	8	6
Major third below	12, 22, 23, 59, 60, 61, 62, 63, 75, 77, 82	11	8
Minor third below	7, 8, 9, 11, 13, 14, 18, 21, 31, 32, 33, 34, 35, 36, 40, 41, 42, 58, 65, 67, 69, 72, 73, 74, 76, 78, 81, 94, 98, 99, 101, 102, 103, 104, 106, 107, 108, 110, 113, 114, 116, 117, 124, 125.	44	34
Whole tone below	44, 55, 64, 80, 111	5	4
Semitone below	2, 92, 121, 129, 130	5	4
Songs containing notes lower than, but not immediately preceding, final note.	18, 19, 26, 45, 46, 47, 50, 54, 56, 66, 79, 86, 87, 90, 115, 118, 120, 127.	18	14
Total		130	......

[1] A portion of these songs contain notes lower than the final note, as well as the lower tone which immediately precedes it.

TABLE 5.—NUMBER OF TONES COMPRISED IN COMPASS OF SONG

	Serial number of songs	Number	Per cent
Compass of—			
10 tones	124	1	......
9 tones	78, 112	2	......
8 tones	31, 33, 39, 50, 54, 61, 65, 75, 79, 80, 87, 94, 97, 114, 129	15	11
7 tones	18, 19, 21, 35, 36, 40, 41, 42, 43, 48, 49, 51, 60, 62, 63, 64, 68, 69, 70, 72, 73, 74, 76, 81, 82, 90, 98, 101, 102, 103, 104, 106, 107, 108, 109, 110, 113, 125, 126, 127.	40	32
6 tones	4, 6, 14, 15, 22, 23, 26, 28, 34, 44, 45, 46, 47, 59, 67, 77, 86, 92, 100, 120, 128, 130.	22	17
5 tones	3, 7, 8, 10, 12, 13, 17, 20, 24, 25, 29, 30, 32, 37, 38, 52, 53, 55, 56, 66, 71, 84, 85, 88, 89, 91, 93, 95, 96, 105, 111, 115, 116, 118, 119, 121.	35	27
4 tones	1, 2, 9, 11, 16, 27, 58, 99, 117	10	7
3 tones	5, 57, 83, 122, 123	5	4
Total		130	......

TABLE 6.—TONE MATERIAL

	Serial number of songs	Number	Per cent
Second 5-toned scale	51, 69, 74, 75, 80, 97, 98, 114, 125	9	7
Fourth 5-toned scale	33, 35, 36, 41, 42, 43, 52, 54, 65, 78, 87, 90, 101, 102, 103, 104, 106, 107, 108, 110.	20	15
Major triad	12, 25, 71	3	2
Major triad and sixth	4, 77	2	1
Major triad and second	39, 84, 88, 89, 91, 119,	6	4
Minor triad and sixth	22, 23	2	1
Minor triad and fourth	7, 8, 9, 13, 24, 32, 37, 59, 113, 115, 116	11	9
Minor triad and second	6, 93, 95, 120	4	3
Octave complete	129	1	-----
Octave complete except seventh	34, 40, 50, 82, 112, 127, 130	7	-----
Octave complete except seventh and one other tone.	15, 17, 18, 19, 28, 44, 46, 53, 60, 61, 62, 63, 85, 92, 96, 100, 105, 111, 118, 128.	20	15
Octave complete except sixth	48, 49, 86, 94	4	3
Octave complete except sixth and one other tone.	21, 26, 124	3	2
Octave complete except fourth	31, 70	2	1
Octave complete except second	45, 64, 67, 76, 126	5	3
Lacking the third	29, 30	2	1
Other combinations of tone	1, 2, 3, 5, 10, 11, 14, 27, 47, 56, 57, 58, 66, 68, 79, 81, 83, 99, 109, 117, 122, 123.	22	17
Irregular in tonality	16, 20, 38, 55, 72, 73, 121	7	5
Total		130	-----

TABLE 7.—ACCIDENTALS

	Serial number of songs	Number	Per cent
Songs containing—			
No accidentals		104	80
Seventh raised	26, 94	2	1
Sixth raised	76, 81	2	1
Fourth raised	37, 46, 64	3	2
Sixth and third raised	118	1	-----
Seventh lowered	44, 67, 68, 70	4	3
Sixth lowered	35, 47, 50, 59, 103, 104	6	5
Fifth lowered	116	1	-----
Irregular	16, 20, 38, 55, 72, 73, 121	7	5
Total		130	-----

TABLE 8.—STRUCTURE

	Serial number of songs	Number	Per cent
Melodic	1, 2, 3, 7, 8, 9, 11, 13, 14, 15, 17, 18, 21, 23, 24, 26, 27, 29, 30, 31, 34, 35, 37, 39, 40, 41, 42, 43, 44, 45, 46, 47, 48, 49, 50, 51, 52, 53, 54, 56, 57, 58, 59, 60, 61, 62, 63, 64, 66, 67, 68, 69, 70, 74, 75, 76, 79, 80, 81, 82, 83, 84, 85, 87, 88, 90, 92, 93, 94, 96, 97, 98, 100, 101, 102, 103, 105, 106, 109, 111, 112, 113, 114, 117, 118, 120, 122, 125, 126, 127, 128, 129, 130.	93	72
Melodic with harmonic framework.	4, 28, 33, 36, 64, 89, 91, 95, 99, 104, 107, 108, 110, 115, 116	15	10
Harmonic	5, 6, 10, 12, 19, 22, 25, 32, 71, 77, 78, 86, 119, 123, 124	15	10
Irregular	16, 20, 38, 55, 72, 73, 121	7	5
Total		130	-----

TABLE 9.—FIRST PROGRESSION—DOWNWARD AND UPWARD

	Serial number of songs	Number	Per cent
Downward	3, 9, 10, 16, 17, 25, 27, 28, 31, 32, 34, 37, 39, 40, 41, 42, 43, 45, 47, 48, 50, 52, 53, 54, 55, 59, 61, 63, 64, 71, 73, 84, 89, 90, 91, 94, 96, 97, 102, 105, 107, 108, 109, 111, 112, 113, 115, 117, 121, 124, 125, 129, 130.	53	40
Upward	1, 2, 4, 5, 6, 7, 8, 11, 12, 13, 14, 15, 18, 19, 20, 21, 22, 23, 24, 26, 29, 30, 33, 35, 36, 38, 44, 46, 49, 53, 56, 57, 58, 60, 62, 65, 66, 67, 68, 69, 70, 72, 74, 75, 76, 77, 78, 79, 80, 81, 82, 83, 85, 86, 87, 88, 92, 93, 95, 98, 99, 100, 101, 103, 104, 106, 110, 114, 116, 118, 119, 120, 122, 123, 126, 127, 128.	77	60
Total		130	------

TABLE 10.—TOTAL NUMBER OF PROGRESSIONS—DOWNWARD AND UPWARD

	Number	Per cent
Downward	3, 215	53
Upward	2, 877	47
Total	6, 092	----------

TABLE 11.—INTERVALS IN DOWNWARD PROGRESSION

	Number	Per cent		Number	Per cent
Interval of a—			Interval of a—Continued.		
Minor sixth	3	------	Major second	1, 455	44
Fifth	34	1	Minor second	177	5
Fourth	292	9			
Major third	349	10	Total	3, 215	------
Minor third	905	30			

TABLE 12.—INTERVALS IN UPWARD PROGRESSION

	Number	Per cent		Number	Per cent
Interval of a—			Interval of a—Continued.		
Octave	4	------	Major third	333	12
Seventh	3	------	Minor third	830	3
Major sixth	6	------	Major second	1, 123	40
Minor sixth	1	------	Minor second	156	6
Fifth	158	6			
Fourth	263	9	Total	2, 877	------

TABLE 13.—AVERAGE NUMBER OF SEMITONES IN AN INTERVAL

Number of songs	130
Number of intervals	6, 092
Number of semitones	17, 697
Average number of semitones in an interval	2. 9

Rhythmic Analysis

Table 14.—PART OF MEASURE ON WHICH SONG BEGINS

	Serial number of songs	Number	Per cent
Beginning on unaccented part of measure.	2, 3, 5, 6, 7, 8, 9, 10, 11, 12, 14, 17, 23, 25, 33, 35, 38, 46, 47, 49, 52, 53, 54, 56, 57, 58, 59, 60, 61, 63, 64, 66, 67, 69, 70, 71, 72, 73, 74, 78, 79, 80, 81, 83, 85, 86, 88, 91, 92, 94, 95, 97, 99, 100, 105, 106, 107, 108, 109, 111, 116, 119, 120, 124, 125, 126, 127, 129.	68	51
Beginning on accented part of measure.	1, 4, 12, 15, 16, 18, 19, 20, 21, 22, 24, 26, 27, 28, 29, 30, 31, 32, 34, 36, 37, 39, 40, 41, 42, 43, 44, 45, 48, 50, 51, 55, 62, 64, 68, 75, 76, 77, 82, 84, 87, 89, 90, 93, 96, 98, 101, 102, 103, 104, 110, 112, 113, 114, 115, 117, 118, 121, 122, 123, 128, 130.	62	49
Total		130	

Table 15.—RHYTHM (METER) OF FIRST MEASURE

First measure in—	Serial number of songs	Number	Per cent
2–4 time	1, 3, 4, 5, 6, 7, 9, 10, 12, 13, 15, 17, 18, 19, 20, 21, 22, 23, 25, 26, 27, 28, 29, 30, 32, 33, 35, 36, 37, 40, 41, 42, 43, 45, 47, 48, 52, 53, 54, 55, 56, 57, 58, 60, 62, 63, 65, 66, 67, 68, 69, 70, 73, 74, 75, 76, 80, 82, 83, 84, 85, 87, 88, 90, 91, 92, 93, 94, 96, 97, 98, 99, 100, 101, 102, 103, 104, 105, 108, 109, 110, 112, 113, 114, 115, 117, 120, 121, 122, 123, 124, 127, 130.	93	71
3–4 time	11, 14, 16, 24, 31, 34, 38, 39, 44, 51, 59, 64, 71, 72, 77, 78, 79, 81, 86, 89, 95, 106, 116, 119, 125, 126, 128, 129.	28	20
5–4 time	2	1	
3–8 time	46, 61, 107	3	2
4–8 time	50	1	
5–8 time	49, 111	2	1
6–8 time	8	1	
7–8 time	118	1	
Total		130	

Table 16.—CHANGE OF TIME (MEASURE-LENGTHS)

	Serial number of songs	Number	Per cent
Songs containing no change of time.	1, 15, 17, 18, 19, 23, 26, 28, 30, 32, 33, 35, 36, 38, 45, 47, 51, 53, 54, 55, 56, 65, 74, 83, 100, 103, 104, 111, 112, 114, 117, 120, 127.	33	26
Songs containing a change of time.	2, 3, 4, 5, 6, 7, 8, 9, 10, 11, 12, 13, 14, 16, 20, 21, 22, 24, 25, 27, 29, 31, 34, 37, 39, 40, 41, 42, 43, 44, 46, 48, 49, 50, 52, 57, 58, 59, 60, 61, 62, 63, 64, 66, 67, 68, 69, 70, 71, 72, 73, 75, 76, 77, 78, 79, 80, 81, 82, 84, 85, 86, 87, 88, 89, 90, 91, 92, 93, 94, 95, 96, 97, 98, 99, 101, 102, 105, 106, 107, 108, 109, 110, 113, 115, 116, 118, 119, 121, 122, 123, 124, 125, 126, 128, 129, 130.	97	74
Total		130	

TABLE 17.—RHYTHMIC PERIOD OR UNIT

	Serial number of songs	Number	Per cent
Songs containing—			
2 rhythmic periods [1]	1, 4, 5, 7, 8, 13, 14, 17, 21, 22, 23, 25, 26, 39, 42, 44, 45, 47, 51, 53, 56, 112, 117, 119.	24	19
3 rhythmic periods	3, 6, 9, 10, 11, 12, 15, 18, 19, 20, 41, 46, 48, 49, 54	15	11
4 rhythmic periods	16, 50, 52	3	2
No rhythmic unit	2, 24, 37, 58, 59, 63, 70, 71, 76, 77, 80, 82, 89, 90, 92, 93, 95, 96, 104, 121, 123, 125.	22	17
1 rhythmic unit	27, 28, 29, 30, 31, 32, 33, 40, 43, 57, 60, 61, 62, 66, 67, 68, 69, 72, 73, 74, 75, 78, 81, 83, 84, 85, 86, 87, 88, 91, 98, 99, 100, 101, 102, 103, 105, 107, 110, 111, 115, 118, 120, 122, 124, 126, 127, 128.	48	37
2 rhythmic units	36, 38, 64, 65, 79, 94, 97, 106, 108, 109, 113, 116, 129, 130	14	10
3 rhythmic units	55, 114	2	1
4 rhythmic units	34, 35	2	1
Total		130	------

[1] The following songs in this and the 2 following groups contain 1 rhythmic unit: 15, 18, 19, 21, 22, 39, 41, 42, 45, 46, 49, 51, 53, 54, 119. The following contain 2 rhythmic units: 17, 44, 47, 50, 56, 112, 117. The following contains 3 rhythmic units: 52.

TABLE 18.—RHYTHM (METER) OF DRUM, RATTLE, AND NASAL ACCOMPANIMENT

	Serial number of songs	Number	Per cent
Songs containing continuous rhythm in accompaniment—			
Rhythm No. 1	4, 5, 6, 9, 10, 11, 33, 34, 49, 51, 52, 54, 56, 77	14	11
Rhythm No. 2	15, 18, 19	3	2
Rhythm No. 3	27, 28, 29, 30, 31, 35, 36, 37, 74, 98	10	7
Rhythm No. 4	99, 101, 102, 104, 106, 108	6	5
Rhythm No. 5	115, 116, 119	3	2
Rhythm No. 6	124, 125	2	1
Songs with accompaniment in quarter-note rhythm with rests.	12, 65, 70, 71, 75, 78, 79, 80, 81, 82	10	7
Songs with accompaniment in other rhythms.	7, 8, 13, 14, 16, 17, 32, 38, 45, 50, 53, 55, 59, 60, 61, 62, 63, 64, 66, 69, 72, 97, 100, 103, 105, 107, 109, 110, 111.	29	22
Recorded without accompaniment.	1, 2, 3, 20, 21, 22, 23, 24, 25, 26, 39, 40, 41, 42, 43, 44, 46, 47, 48, 57, 58, 67, 68, 73, 76, 83, 84, 85, 86, 87, 88, 89, 90, 91, 92, 93, 94, 95, 96, 112, 113, 114, 117, 118, 120, 121, 122, 123, 126, 127, 128, 129, 130.	53	40
Total		130	------

Rhythms in the accompaniment of
more than one song

Also quarter notes with rests corresponding to rests of voice.

AUTHORITIES CITED

CULIN, STEWART. Games of the North American Indians. Twenty-fourth Ann. Rept. Bur. Amer. Ethn., Washington, 1907.

DENSMORE, FRANCES. Chippewa Music. Bull. 45, Bur. Amer. Ethn., Washington, 1910.

——— Chippewa Music—II. Bull. 53, Bur. Amer. Ethn., Washington, 1913.

——— Teton Sioux Music. Bull. 61, Bur. Amer. Ethn., Washington, 1918.

——— Northern Ute Music. Bull. 75, Bur. Amer. Ethn., Washington, 1922.

——— Mandan and Hidatsa Music. Bull. 80, Bur. Amer. Ethn., Washington, 1923.

——— Music of the Tule Indians of Panama. Smithsonian Inst., Misc. Colls., vol. 77, no. 11 (Publ. 2864), Washington, 1926.

——— Papago Music. Bull. 90, Bur. Amer. Ethn., Washington, 1929.

——— Pawnee Music. Bull. 93, Bur. Amer. Ethn., Washington, 1929.

——— Menominee Music. Bull. 102, Bur. Amer. Ethn., Washington, 1931.

DOCUMENTOS PARA LA HISTORIA DE MEXICO. Four series. 20 vols. Mexico, 1853–1857.

FOX STRANGWAYS, A. H. Music of Hindostan. Oxford, 1914.

GIFFORD, E. W. The Kamia of Imperial Valley, Bull. 97, Bur. Amer. Ethn., Washington, 1931.

HANDBOOK OF AMERICAN INDIANS NORTH OF MEXICO. Edited by F. W. Hodge, Bur. Amer. Ethn., Bull. 30, pts. 1–2, Washington, 1907–1910.

HENSHAW, H. W. [Article] Yuman Family. In Handbook of Amer. Inds., Bur. Amer. Ethn., Bull. 30, pt. 2, pp. 1011–1012, Washington, 1910.

HERZOG, GEORGE. The Yuman Musical Style. Journ. Amer. Folk-Lore, vol. 41, pp. 183–231, New York, 1928.

HRDLIČKA, ALEŠ. Notes on the Indians of Sonora, Mexico. Amer. Anthrop., n. s. vol. VI, pp. 51–89, Lancaster, Pa., 1904.

KROEBER, A. L. Handbook of the Indians of California. Bur. Amer. Ethn., Bull. 78, Washington, 1925.

PUTNAM, G. R. A Yuma Cremation. Amer. Anthrop., vol. VIII, pp. 264–267. Washington, 1895.

INDEX

○